A HYPOCRITE'S GUIDE TO AUTHENTICITY **Tim Baker**

ZONDERVAN®

ZONDERVAN.com/
AUTHORTRACKER
follow your favorite authors

ZONDERVAN

Jesus Is for Liars: A Hypocrite's Guide to Authenticity
Copyright © 2009 by Tim Baker

This title is also available as a Zondervan ebook.
Visit www.zondervan.com/ebooks.

Requests for information should be addressed to:

Zondervan, *Grand Rapids, Michigan* 49530

Library of Congress Cataloging-in-Publication Data

Baker, Tim, 1965-
    Jesus is for liars : a hypocrite's guide to authenticity / by Tim Baker.
      p. cm.
   ISBN 978-0-310-28363-8 (pbk.)
    1. Christian teenagers—Religious life. I. Title.
  BV4531.3.B34 2010

  248.8'3—dc22   2009044666

Interior design by Mark Novelli, IMAGO

Printed in the United States of America

09 10 11 12 13 14 15 • 18 17 16 15 14 13 12 11 10 9 8 7 6 5 4 3 2 1

For those who aren't afraid to consider that God might not be exactly what we've always expected.

CONTENTS

ACKNOWLEDGMENTS

A Christian book about spiritual authenticity is almost certainly one of two things. Either it's the writer's perspective on what it takes to be, for lack of a better phrase, "just like Jesus," or it's a reaction to everything that writer has ever been taught or been living. The book you're holding is more the second one. I'm not trying to tell *you* how to live as much as I'm reflecting on how I've lived and thought about God, and what we can learn from that.

So I'd like to say *hi* and *thanks* to all the people who have helped make me the person I am today. Thanks to all those who have shaped my theology and have listened to me talk through my ideas about God and my thoughts about Christianity. There have been a lot of you...hundreds of students and many friends. You know how I tend to think with my mouth and not with my head, so...thanks for listening to me think. You know who you are.

My family has sacrificed so much as I've written this book. It's taken me about a year to sort out my thoughts, and in that time, I've ignored my kids way too much and taken my wife for granted far too often. So thanks to Jacqui, Nicole, Jessica, and Jacob for letting me go for just a bit to write down some thoughts on spirituality. Kids, I hope these ideas will fuel your walk with Jesus.

A Christian book about spiritual authenticity is almost certainly one of two things. Either it's the writer's perspective on what it takes to be, for lack of a better phrase, "just like Jesus," or it's a reaction to everything that writer has ever been taught or been living. The book you're holding is more the second one. I'm not trying to tell *you* how to live as much as I'm reflecting on how I've lived and thought about God, and what we can learn from that.

So I'd like to say *hi* and *thanks* to all the people who have helped make me the person I am today. Thanks to all those who have shaped my theology and have listened to me talk through my ideas about God and my thoughts about Christianity. There have been a lot of you...hundreds of students and many friends. You know how I tend to think with my mouth and not with my head, so...thanks for listening to me think. You know who you are.

My family has sacrificed so much as I've written this book. It's taken me about a year to sort out my thoughts, and in that time, I've ignored my kids way too much and taken my wife for granted far too often. So thanks to Jacqui, Nicole, Jessica, and Jacob for letting me go for just a bit to write down some thoughts on spirituality. Kids, I hope these ideas will fuel your walk with Jesus.

I don't have an office, so I probably ought to thank the places I've "officed" while writing this book. Thanks to Carl's Jr, Arby's, Roxie's Café, Wendy's, The Java Lounge, the Downtown Coffee Café, a few hotels, and the many other places that have let me sit and write for hours. It's probably a good idea for me to thank coffee in general, since I consumed nearly an entire field of beans while I wrote this book.

Book editors serve as invisible servants. You never know they're there, and if you're ever reading a book and notice the hand of an editor, you've just read the work of a very bad editor. My friend Doug Davidson is easily the best book editor I've ever worked with. Doug and I shared lunch at the Fort Worth Stockyards when we were nearly done with this book. We ate Dirty Burgers, swatted at bees, and enjoyed some root beer and good music. Doug...I love you, and not just because you rock out on lead guitar. Thanks for all the gentle coaxing and hard work. If this book reads right, it's because you worked your caboose off.

Youth Specialties was kind enough to buy this book based solely on the idea, and in the process of completing this book they have been wonderful. Roni Meek, you've been patient beyond patient. And Jay Howver, thanks for listening to this and buying into it. You YS folks know what you're doing, and I'm thankful you've allowed me to contribute to your good work.

And finally...you, the reader. I want to acknowledge the role you've played in my process of writing this book. We've never met, but knowing that you'd be reading these words has had a profound impact on what I've said. I've tried to be careful, to not say too much bad stuff, to build in the right amount of God-stuff so you know I'm a Christian, but also enough other stuff to help you understand that the word *Christian* doesn't really answer all the questions about what it means to follow Jesus.

Thanks for the time you're investing in reading this. Feel free to chat back to me about what you've read. Email me at tim@timbaker.cc, or connect with me on Facebook.com/timbaker1.

CHAPTER
THE UNATTAINABLY PERFECT FAITH
ONE

At a time when most American churches are on a journey toward bigger, better, and more expensive, our church is small. I guess we have about 150 people most Sundays. Our worship music is typically a blend of traditional songs and choruses, backed by our very skilled piano player, a talented bass player, and a few other musicians. The preaching is good, but probably fairly typical. We are not cutting edge. We're not heavy on drama, and we don't invest in those catchy worship movies. We are not emotional. We talk a lot before and after worship, but we're pretty quiet during the service. In fact, if anyone's talking during the service (other than the preacher), it's probably me. I'm the usher who asks about your week as I pass you the offering plate. I'll talk to you while I'm passing you the body of Jesus or the blood of Christ. I am not particularly outgoing, but in this quiet, introverted environment, I'm often the life of the party.

We recently rearranged our worship seating into a circle. It was an effort to help all these introverts look at one another while worshipping and celebrating communion, recognizing that we are, in fact, the body of Christ. I thought this was a great idea, at least in theory. But on one particular morning recently, the change wasn't working for me. Maybe I was just tired; I'd been up late the night before. But I felt terribly uncomfortable looking at everyone singing and taking communion. I was not into the moment—mentally, emotionally, or spiritually. The more the service went on, the more I didn't want to be there. I imagined myself running from the room, screaming in frustration and anger because I wasn't connecting, tipping old ladies over and knocking down children in my desperate attempt to leave the Jesus Arena.

> OUR SPIRITUAL JOURNEYS SHOULD BE FOCUSED ONLY ON GOD, BUT OFTEN WE'RE DISTRACTED BY OTHER BELIEVERS. WHEN HAVE YOU FACED THIS?

During one hymn a good friend, someone I deeply respect, came over, threw his arm around me, and whispered, "What's wrong with you? Are you okay?" I guess he'd noticed I wasn't clapping along or singing loudly or whatever. Maybe he could see my eyes dancing around as I tired to figure a way out of the room without embarrassing myself or ruining the moment for anyone else. Immediately, I felt guilty, like I'd committed a sin and made God angry, because I wasn't floating down the same spiritual river as the rest of the congregation that day.

I felt that guilt for a millisecond, and then I had a flash of understanding about my journey of faith. It was like a light bulb went on, and I finally understood that my spiritual journey wasn't the same as my friend's journey—or that of anyone else in the room that day. I didn't feel like standing and clapping that morning...is that okay? In fact, I might even want to skip a month of worship services...will God still love me? What if those lyrics printed on the Day-Glo white screen make no sense to me or don't connect with where I am in that moment? Am I wrong to feel that way? Are we all included in the body of Christ, whether we clap along to the praise songs or not? Is it okay if my spiritual journey includes potholes?

We Christians talk so much about how "It's great that we are all different in the Body of Christ," but sometimes I wonder if we really believe it. Sometimes I think we Christians don't care as much about being like Christ as we care about being *like one another.* Our desire isn't a Christ-centered uniqueness, it's a churchy sameness. We think we're okay only if we look, talk, and act like everyone else we know who follows God. We claim the *idea* of uniqueness and spiritual individuality, but we don't really believe it.

But, in that moment, my focus on outward appearances and trying to fit in was suddenly made clear to me. I felt saddened by all the time and energy and guilt I'd spent trying to measure up to someone else's idea of what a good Christian would look and act like. I wasn't angry about my friend's question about whether I was "okay"—but I was angry about who I'd been, what I'd been ashamed about, what had motivated my spiritual guilt. I understood that my spiritual journey isn't about my being like my friend, or like my pastor, or like you—it's about my being like Jesus. It's about pursuing God passionately and personally. If my love for Jesus is going to be genuine, then it has to be genuinely mine. It can't be like your love for Jesus or like that of the person sitting next to me in worship. The only spiritual ideal is Jesus; the only call is to be like him. There is no other spiritual calling.

I threw my arm around my friend, bent over close to his ear, and said, "Nope, nothing's wrong with me. Is there something wrong with you?" Apparently, there wasn't.

I didn't mean to be rude. I guess I could have apologized and tried to explain what was happening in me. But I needed, in that moment, simply to realize and accept that my spirituality is my own. There was nothing wrong with me as I just stood there silently, just as there was nothing wrong with him as he continued clap-clap-clapping along to all these catchy Jesus love songs.

My friend stood next to me for a few minutes, clapping high in the air. I think he was hoping I'd see his clapping as encouragement and start clapping along. Before long, he went back to sit with his wife, and I felt incredibly empowered. It was a moment where I deeply understood that my quest to be God's is exactly that...a quest. And, more than that, it is *my* quest, and

> THINK ABOUT A TIME YOU FELT LIKE YOU HAD TO MEASURE UP TO SOMEONE ELSE'S SPIRITUAL IDEAL. WHAT EFFECT DID THAT HAVE ON YOU?

by those words, I mean I own the path I choose. I am responsible for my own journey with all its mistakes and successes. I am in love with God, and I will pursue him in my own unique way, the way he has made me. And that might mean I will stand when others sit, I'll laugh when others cry, and I'll kneel at all the wrong moments—I may even do word search games during the sermon. I don't have to pretend to be anyone else. God loves me, and God can use me, just as I am.

PERFECTION VS. HONESTY

I think this focus on appearances, this desire to live in a way that doesn't ruffle any feathers, is something a lot of us Christians struggle with. And I believe one reason for this struggle is an assumption that we need to be perfect in how we follow Jesus. We get the idea that all the people in Scripture—guys like Luke and Peter and Paul who model what it means to follow Jesus for us—were perfect. Preachers hold up these disciples as shining examples. When we believe (wrongly, by the way) that the people in Scripture had their entire lives together, we start to think we must be inadequate. So we try to cover it up by pretending to be what we think we're supposed to be. We start reading Scripture with an us-and-them mentality. We read about Peter's evangelism or Timothy's pastoring, and we wonder why we're not perfect like that. Why aren't we performing more miracles? Why aren't all our prayers answered? Why aren't we more like these pictures we have of the heroes of our faith?

My story is not the tale of a spiritual superhero. Sometime I hunger for God with great passion—but often I don't. My walk with God is riddled with lost attempts. I try to stay deeply connected with God, but I fail over and over. I do my best to participate in spiritual disciplines, but I fail at that too. Sometimes prayer feels like an empty promise and "worship" is no more than bland attendance. Even committed relationships head for the shallow end of the pool, where no one shares their real lives. And I feel like a failure.

But I think the truth is that the heroes of Scripture struggled every bit as much as I do. Think about Peter. He was Jesus' right hand man—the "rock" on which Jesus said he would build his church (Matthew 16:18). Yet Peter messes up as often as he succeeds. He's always getting it wrong and missing the point of Jesus' words. He steps out onto the water in faith—and immediately starts sinking. And with the shadow of the cross looming, he denies he ever even knew Jesus. And not just once. Peter denies it three separate times.

WHAT UNHEALTHY MODELS OF SPIRITUAL PERFECTION HAVE YOU TRIED TO ADOPT INTO YOUR LIFE? HOW HAS THIS AFFECTED YOUR WALK WITH GOD?

Or take Paul. This guy wrote half the New Testament and founded countless churches. But check out what he says about his own spiritual life here in Romans 7:14-25:

> We know that the law is spiritual; but I am unspiritual, sold as a slave to sin. I do not understand what I do. For what I want to do I do not do, but what I hate I do...I know that good itself does not dwell in me, that is, in my sinful nature. For I have the desire to do what is good, but I can-

not carry it out. For I do not do the good I want to do, but the evil I do not want to do—this I keep on doing. Now if I do what I do not want to do, it is no longer I who do it, but it is sin living in me that does it.

So I find this law at work: Although I want to do good, evil is right there with me. For in my inner being I delight in God's law; but I see another law at work in me, waging war against the law of my mind and making me a prisoner of the law of sin at work within me. What a wretched man I am! Who will rescue me from this body of death? Thanks be to God, who delivers me through Jesus Christ our Lord!

This is a guy who knows he's not perfect. If Paul showed up at the next church potluck, I'm not sure any of us would choose to sit next to him. I bet he wouldn't be accepted in most churches, and I *know* he'd never get hired by any church that did a background check. And Peter...if he were in our churches, he'd be that stumbling failure of a believer the rest of us were always praying for. What about the rest of our biblical superheroes? We'd kick Abraham out of our churches for acting like Sarah wasn't his wife, give Noah the boot for getting drunk and laying around naked, and toss out David for sleeping with another guy's wife and having her husband killed.

This mixture of a desire to do good and a tendency to do evil is normal. Our frustration that we are not spiritual heroes is to be expected. Our insides waging war against God's law is normal, too. Paul's words and the struggles of these other biblical heroes don't make our failures okay, but they give the struggle legs, they put meat on its bones.

Paul's words also lift a huge weight off our shoulders. His words are a reminder that the call to spirituality *isn't* a call to perfection. It isn't a call to become someone we're not, to pretend to be different than we are. We aren't in this race against anyone else. We're not *in it to win it*. And even though a lot of contemporary Christianity focuses on doing stuff, this call that Paul opens our minds to is not a call to do anything. It's a call to be ourselves—a call to be spiritual the way we were created to be spiritual.

> IF YOU COULD BE SPIRITUAL IN THE UNIQUE WAY YOU WERE DESIGNED TO BE, WHAT WOULD THAT LOOK LIKE?

A CALL TO AUTHENTICITY

Just a few months ago, I was in Mexico, on a mission trip with students. We were there for a lot of reasons—to try to help the people in that poverty-stricken community, to lead small children into a better understanding of who God is, to pray with and for people, and to learn what it's like to live in another culture. Throughout that week, I felt God leading me to read the Sermon on the Mount, that famous speech where Jesus covered all of the basics of the Law—leading some listeners to believe he was trying to toss out the Law, and others to believe he understood it more deeply than any other teacher before.

As I read that great sermon from Matthew's gospel over and over, I began to feel like Jesus' words about the hypocrisy of the religious leaders of his day were directed right to me. I'd not been the kind of man I'd always thought I was. My actions were often just a carefully constructed veneer that was modeled on what I thought a Christian was supposed to think and do. It was a lot of well-intentioned pretending.

Each day in Mexico, when I got up early and read my Bible (something I hadn't done regularly in years, despite all my talk about how much I love the Bible), I felt an inescapable call from Christ, a challenge to live differently. I noticed the difference between what I do and what motivates what I do. Jesus' words rang out clearly in my heart, a reminder that what I'd been doing with my hands and my feet, the physical me, didn't matter as much as the attitude that motivated the movement of my hands and feet. His words in those passages were focused on our hearts, our intent, and our honesty. As I read those words I understood that God loves me but is frustrated with my pharisaical outward spirituality, which, in the end, is motivated by an inauthentic heart. I understood that I'd been spending my energy trying to get in sync with other believers rather than in sync with God. Of course, Jesus' call to be more compassionate and more humble rang out loud and clear as I read that sermon. But, in every reading, the cry to be honest about who I am and how I live was even louder.

I believe Jesus exemplified the kind of life we ought to live. The entirety of the Scriptures points to Jesus' call to live like this. Be holy like this. Jesus shows us not only everything that God is, but also everything we need to be, all we aspire to be spiritually.

But this portrait of Jesus that we love so much, the one that Scripture gives us, has been painted over so many times. It's been touched up by tradition. It's been graffitied by prosperity preachers. It's been commoditized by marketers who want to sell a McJesus spirituality. It's been marred by theological frameworks and guilt. It's been gooed up by the shallow theology found on the shelves of Christian bookstores, the simplistic slogans on Christian t-shirts, and the stuff you find on cheesy Christian web pages. The real Jesus is still there, but he's tough to see. It's like our churches have dressed Jesus up in a suit and tie, so he looks suspiciously like a successful American businessman rather than a radical prophet who shook up the world. How do we know how to follow him authentically? How do we even know who the real Jesus is? He's certainly there, but he's buried under centuries of other people's thoughts about who he is.

> WHAT DOES JESUS' SPIRITUALITY LOOK LIKE TO YOU? WHAT OF HIS LIFE IN GOD CAN YOU IMITATE? HOW WOULD IMITATING JESUS CHANGE WHO YOU ARE RIGHT NOW?

Christian authenticity is simply this: It is the search for the real Jesus, and it is the attempt to be who we truly are in his presence. We have to want this honesty and integrity before God if we are going to be spiritually authentic. I struggle to reach through the marketing to discover who he was. And in those moments when I get a glimpse of the real Jesus, I can't seem to get away from my own flaws. My life doesn't always look—maybe it doesn't *ever* look—like the kind of life I think Jesus wants from me. I'm filled with conflict—there's the part of me that loves Scripture, but another part that doesn't allow it to make a big enough difference to really change who I am. Instead of being honest about my struggles and doubts and questions and failures, I try to paint over all the warts and mistakes and missteps. I try to give you the impression that I've got it all together.

THE LOVE OF GOD SHOULD BE A MOTIVATING FORCE IN OUR AUTHENTIC SPIRITUALITY. WHAT CAN YOU DO TODAY TO EMBRACE GOD'S PASSIONATE LOVE FOR YOU? HOW WOULD EMBRACING HIS LOVE IN YOU CHANGE YOUR SPIRITUAL HONESTY?

This is hypocrisy, and it's become my shield and my hiding place, the primary theme of my pursuit of God. No matter how much I want to live the way Scripture teaches and no matter how strong my passion to be godly, it's impossible. So I cover that impossible journey with the shield of what I think the church expects me to be. I play the role of the good Christian. I embrace theological beliefs that don't always make sense to me. I don't use bad words. I sit through worship services on days when I'd rather be somewhere else. I do all this to convince you that I'm normal, that I'm okay, that I'm acceptable. And in doing that, I end up feeling like I'm living a lie. Why can't we just be honest? What is there to lose?

Here's what I'm discovering in all of this: Jesus is for liars. He knows who we are, and he accepts us anyway. We don't have to pretend to be someone else. We don't have to try to live up to anyone else's idea of what a proper Christian is supposed to think, do, or look like.

So let's shed a spirituality that searches for truth on the Internet. Let's not live a secondhand faith, one we have inherited from our parents or friends. Let's stop building our belief in God on fads or slogans.

Let's commit together to be honest about who we are and what we're going through. When we are empty and dry, we will say so. When we have hit a rough spot in our walk with God, we will tell someone and not paint over it. Let's admit that we struggle with being wholly God's and allow ourselves the beautiful honesty that our spirituality is our own. It does not have to mimic someone else's.

Is it possible to combine our *desire* to be like Christ with our skillful *ability* to live totally counter to that? Can God create in us a new creation, synergized with his power? Can God use our desire to be like him while understanding our ability to break promises? Does he really have a use for those of us who can't stand cheesy Christianity? Is it possible to follow Jesus and not feel like we have to perform? Can we live authentic Christian lives without feeling we must beat ourselves with barbed wire whenever we fall short?

Join with me in letting go of the unattainable perfect faith. Let's let go of the expectations others have for us and move together toward an authentic faith that works inside each of us in its own unique way, and then moves out from us, finding strong legs in the real world.

CHAPTER
THINGS ON THE SURFACE
TWO

The moment I saw the doll in his backseat, I knew there was going to be trouble. But let me back up just a bit.

When I was a kid, it took a lot for God to get my attention. *A lot.* There was noise in my life coming from many directions. My parents' divorce and their becoming new people and their new dating relationships. My anger at having two homes and four parents. My passion for BMX bike racing. Not to mention all the normal adolescent transitions and struggles every teenager goes through. There was a whole lot going on.

The seed for my love of God had been planted by our babysitter years earlier, but it was a youth worker who watered that seed one summer, who tended it like it was his own and made sure it grew. I loved him like a dad or my brother or both. I really only knew him for three months, but I learned a lot from him. I learned the secret to running long distances without too much training (run slow, talk deeply). I learned how to keep socks together with their mates (safety pins). And I learned about *Poltergeist*.

The night before I found that doll sitting in his car, we'd gone out to eat. It was my gift to him, because he meant so much, and time with him was worth far more to me than the *Mad* magazines I normally spent my cash on. I told him I'd take him anywhere he wanted to go to eat—and he picked the place I would have chosen. We were a lot alike and shared a love for good hamburgers. Some of the best burgers were an hour away in Columbus, the big city where you went if you really wanted to celebrate. So we went, we ate, and then found ourselves asking the "What's next?" question you ask when you're not ready for the night to end.

He grabbed a newspaper and we decided. *Poltergeist*, the movie. It was new back then, and it was a fabulous exploration into terror and evil spirits...a world I'd been floating near the edges of. We made a quick call to my mom, who said it was okay—but was it *really* okay? Wasn't this movie about everything God was not? Was it not okay? Right or wrong hung in the balance for just a moment, with both winning the battle. We decided to go see it, agreeing that we'd make it an educational event, by committing to talk afterward about the contents of the movie and the feelings evoked in us.

If you've ever seen the movie, you know—it opens doors. At least it did in me back then. Mostly, it opened a fun new door of fear in me. I realized that I *love* scary movies. Movie fear isn't like real fear. When it came to movies, I could be terribly scared and laughing at the same time. Two-dimensional experiences don't equal three-dimensional life, and I knew that. And that's probably one reason I could enjoy the experience of being so terrified.

My favorite scene from the movie was when the son's much loved clown doll is taken over by the spirits of the house, changing from a laughable friend to a demonic attacker. It grabs and attacks the boy, dragging him under the bed. It was terrifying. As I watched, I thought of the stuff at home in my own room that could attack me if a poltergeist were to invade. Except, of course, I believed in Jesus, and I knew that if poltergeists really existed, then Jesus could probably take care of them. So I was safe.

So that next day, when I got into the car after our lunch and found the doll in my seat, it made me scream with terror. His laughing was probably more evil than it should have been. I felt angry and jealous, wishing I'd pranked him before he got to me.

My world was simpler before I met Jesus. Anything that gave you a thrill, as long as it didn't hurt you, was okay. But, somewhere along the line, someone told me that the thrill I got from scary movies was not godly, and it hindered my spirituality. It made God mad at me.

But that didn't make me like scary movies less. It just made me feel guilty about liking them. And, to be honest, that guilt is focused more on what others think about my enjoyment of these films than what I believe God thinks about it. In the same way, I don't use certain words—but it's not so much because I think God finds them inappropriate, but because I know that other believers might hear me and draw conclusions about what kind of Christian I am. So much of my life has involved avoiding certain behavior because of what others might think, and not because of how God might feel.

I think we all do this to some extent. We do and do not do things because of how others might react. And while we do bear some responsibility for how other Christians are influenced by our decisions, in the end, trying to live out of that space becomes a trap filled with unrealistic expectations and unfounded rules. It's silly, and yet, it is so often the blood that pulses through our Christian conduct.

> HOW MUCH OF WHAT YOU DO—AND DON'T DO—IS MOTIVATED BY THE REACTIONS OTHER CHRISTIANS MIGHT HAVE?

PERFORMANCE ART FOR JESUS

This is one of the first areas where this whole question of living authentically gets all mixed up. For too many Christians the beauty of loving Jesus with our lives has been reduced to a bunch of dos and don'ts, a list of rules we are supposed to follow. These rules make us focus only on the surface, the stuff we can see in one another. Our life of faith becomes performance art.

We get concerned about the stuff we see others do or say, and if they aren't living the way we think good Christians should, we form Frankenstein search parties to hunt them down. If people don't dress right, speak right, smell right, act right...if they don't read and watch what we watch and agree with the political perspective of "the rest of us," we chase them out of the Jesus Club.

Now it's natural that we should expect that following Jesus would make some difference in people's behavior. If somebody is walking around drunk all the time and sleeping with someone different every night, that person might claim to be Christ's, but the lifestyle doesn't match that claim. In so many cases, God's biblical guidance makes it clear what kind of people we are to become and how we are called to live. The God who loves us so much wants us to live in ways that clearly reflect that love.

But when we lose sight of God's love as our motivation, when we trust human rules instead of God's guidelines, our lives become performance art. Our authentic struggle gets ruined when "living a life rooted in God's love" is replaced with "living a life *that doesn't get other Christians talking about you.*"

That contrast and struggle of all this performing can leave us in a very lonely place. We know that if we are authentic, if we express our struggles honestly, we risk people talking about us. Nothing kills authenticity more than knowing that people are watching you and expecting you to act or talk a certain way. The pressure to act the way others expect a Christian to act is often more pressure than just wanting to be the kind of person Jesus expects us to be.

Sometimes I wonder what our relationships with Jesus would look like if we weren't all performing the "proper Christian" dance for each other, if each of us were simply loving Jesus because we want to, in the way we long to. What if we truly weren't concerned about how others might react to our lives in Christ? Is fear about what others might say the thing that keeps us devoted to God? Or is our constant concern about how others view our lives a barrier that keeps us from truly loving God?

If we are going to live our faith with authenticity, one of the first things we have to do is decide where we are going to set our eyes. We can choose to look at those around us, notice their flaws and their inability to follow God's laws or our rules, and worry about what they think of us. Or we can focus our eyes—and really, focus our entire selves—on Christ.

HOW WOULD YOUR SPIRITUAL JOURNEY BE DIFFERENT IF YOU FOCUSED ONLY ON GLORIFYING GOD AND DIDN'T WORRY ABOUT THE EXPECTATIONS OF OTHER BELIEVERS?

Maybe it's a little like sailing a boat at night. If you're sailing at night, watching the waves isn't going to help you much, and neither is watching the lights of the other boats. But keeping an eye on the stars will certainly guide you. Keeping our eyes on Christ helps keep our focus off the silly things on the surface, the stuff we often think matters so much. Fixing our eyes on Christ can help us find the right course and keep us focused on the stuff that matters much more.

But even if we keep our eyes on Christ, there's still the challenge of our relationship with the world that surrounds us. We struggle with this tension between the spirit and the flesh, between the godly and the worldly, between the desire to rock out in the world and the desire to worship in the presence of Jesus.

Jesus understood that we would have to live that

tension. Consider these words from John 15, which Jesus spoke to his disciples shortly before he returned to his Father:

> If the world hates you, keep in mind that it hated me first. If you belonged to the world, it would love you as its own. As it is, you do not belong to the world, but I have chosen you out of the world. That is why the world hates you. (John 15:18-19)

The same theme appears two chapters later, as Jesus prays for his followers:

> I have given them your word and the world has hated them, for they are not of the world any more than I am of the world. My prayer is not that you take them out of the world but that you protect them from the evil one. They are not of the world, even as I am not of it. Sanctify them by the truth; your word is truth. As you sent me into the world, I have sent them into the world. (John 17:14-18)

These words are the foundation for the well-known Christian call to be "in the world but not of the world." We've all heard these words. But why is this such a struggle? Why does our effort to live for God "in this world" in ways that are not "of this world" so quickly devolve into living in ways that are not true to who we are?

I think Jesus understood that we'd be torn between the desire to love him with our entire lives and a desire for what the world has to offer; that's normal. We want the stuff, the glitz, the things that make us feel really, really good. We will always be drawn to that stuff, we'll always have our eyes on it. The truth is that there really isn't just one person inside each of us. There are two different people: The person attached to this world (our human person) and the person attached to the spiritual world (our soul person). We are both spirit and flesh, two beings packed in one form. At times we feel like those two sides are at war.

Even though Jesus told us that life in this world will be a challenge, we don't want to admit that we're struggling. We don't want to admit how drawn we are to the world.

But two things happen when we refuse to admit that we are struggling with our connectedness to this world. First of all, we begin to live our lives behind a mask. We live lives that are passionately inauthentic. We spend all our time trying to play the role of a good Christians. We perform for others and lie about who we really are.

That refusal to be honest about the ways we struggle with the world leads to a second problem: We develop a tremendous fear of the world. I'll admit it…fear has been one of the motivating factors in my life as a believer. I've allowed it to rule over me and to prevent me from really living. Now I'm not talking about fear of God, or even fear of other people. I'm talking about fear of the world. I've seen it in my life, and in the lives of others, too. We don't want to become worldly, so we live in fear of the world around us. We don't go anywhere where we might be touched by the world. The world is uncertain; it doesn't follow the definitions we're familiar with. So we avoid it. We venture into that scary place only to tell people about God, and then we flee it like people running from the monster in those old Godzilla movies. We define ourselves by what we don't do: We don't listen to this kind of music; we don't go to these movies; we avoid these places; we're never seen with these people.

But Jesus never tells us to cloister ourselves away from the world. I'm reminded that Jesus didn't walk around cities; he walked through them. He didn't escape the marketplace; he entered it. He didn't avoid the world; he engaged the world. When we lock ourselves away from everything that's happening in the world, the result is a group of people who are out of touch with the stuff we need to know to better present Jesus. When we don't know the language of media, the current texture of music, the incredible moodiness of cinema, the potent power of context and language, we become the ineffective filler in a world searching for meaning. Try as hard as we might, a church that's completely lost touch with the world will never effectively reach into the souls of the people who need to hear God's truth.

FINDING A FILTER

So we can't be cloistered, but we don't want to damage our souls. What's the line?

What if we agreed to hold the world and everything in it with "holy gloves," as if the world were made of sacred shards of broken glass? What if we were intent on discovering God's beauty in this broken world? What if we were willing to explore how it tastes and smells and looks and sounds, trying to find its inner meaning and inner content? What if we remained on a constant search to better understand the world, a relentless pursuit for the presence of God in it, with a desire to be God's redemptive voice within it? What if we opened everything, evaluated everything, were conversant with every idea and concept? What if we loved God's redemptive truth so much that our desire to find it in this world and share it with others was greater than our fear of what we might uncover in the process? Wouldn't it be the coolest thing if every believer were living in this way? Wouldn't it help remove judgment from the Christian life? Couldn't that be a powerful rallying point for believers?

IN WHAT WAYS HAVE YOU CLOISTERED YOURSELF AWAY FROM THE WORLD? HOW HAS THIS HELPED YOUR FAITH? HOW HAS IT HURT IT?

Just as Jesus' words guide us in being aware of our presence in the world, Paul offers us words that can guide us as we handle the stuff we find in this broken world:

> Finally, brothers and sisters, whatever is true, whatever is noble, whatever is right, whatever is pure, whatever is lovely, whatever is admirable—if anything is excellent or praiseworthy—think about such things. Whatever you have learned or received or heard from me, or seen in me—put it into practice. And the God of peace will be with you. (Philippians 4:8-9)

Could it be as simple as Paul makes it sound here? This is the filter we use as we live our lives in this world. The stuff on Paul's list is the stuff our souls should migrate toward, the stuff we should let fill us. Instead of a list of things we should never do, Paul creates a list of things we are invited to pursue. Paul encourages us to go into the world and find those lovely things. He urges us to go out and find truth. He invites us to seek the things that are praiseworthy.

There's no hint here that Paul wants us to live from within some protective bubble of irrelevant churchianity. Paul encourages us to go out into the world that Christ loved and seek out those praiseworthy things in the same way a bird searches for a piece of bread. His list encourages us to be people who are always on the lookout for the lovely, not on a search party to find people who aren't obeying our human-created standards.

Paul's words leave us with authentic questions to ask ourselves as we live each day. Does the music we listen to agree with this passage? Do the movies we watch fill our minds with true and noble thoughts? Do the books we read help fill our minds with praiseworthy thoughts? Truly, such a life moves way beyond performance art and steps squarely into the world of our relationship with Jesus. What we do in Christ cannot be for others; our lives have to be lived for him. And, to that end, what are we doing to enhance that? Are we living in ways that take in the pure and lovely, filtering out that which is destructive? Or are we an open door, allowing other things entrance to our souls, allowing them to corrupt what is rightfully his? Do we let the things of the world diminish who we are in him? Or do we allow our world with care, evaluating it so we can grow and learn more about who we are in him?

And in the midst of all that struggle—as we worry that the world is corrupting our souls and as we desire to live wholly for Jesus—one of the most profound commitments we can make is to be honest with on another about our lives. To quit pretending. If we are having a rotten day, we ought to feel the freedom to say how we feel. If we are hurting, our commitment to honesty should lead us to talk about it. Our struggles and joys shouldn't be sanitized versions of the reality we are living. They should be an honest sharing of what we're facing. We should not live our lives in secret, hiding the ugly stuff from one another. We should be living it honestly, telling the truth about everything, sharing with others our real lives, not the lives we wish we were leading. And with that honesty must come a commitment to support one another. No matter what the story, no matter what the struggle, no matter how deep or trivial the issue might seem to be, we must honor other people's honesty and encourage one another.

Do you hear accountability in that? I hope so. I know...sometimes the idea that others will hold us accountable can cause us to be less than honest. We're reluctant to talk about our real struggles because we don't want to give others access to the parts of our lives we dislike. We don't want to give others permission to ask about those areas of struggle, to check in on us. I think this is one of those things we have to hold in tension: We need to live our lives authentically for God—not to win the approval of others. And yet, we do need to give others whom we trust access to our inner lives and what's really going on. We need to let them ask us those tough questions like, "How does this struggle affect how you see God?" and "Does this behavior create a wall between you and the God who loves you?" and

"Does what you are doing help you grow and be more like Christ?" If we're going to get beyond surface issues, we need safe people who will make the journey with us and ask these honest questions.

FAST FORWARD

It's been 25 years since I found that doll on the seat of my friend's car. Now I'm the youth worker—the seed-watering, Jesus-encouraging person, who's trying to help teenagers grow into the people God wants the to be. Hopefully, I'm a lot like my old mentor—as intuitive and available and life-shaping for others as he was for me.

WHAT DO YOU NEED TO BE MORE HONEST ABOUT IN YOUR WALK WITH GOD? WHOM CAN YOU TRUST WITH THIS HONESTY?

Recently I was having lunch with a student who's also a good friend when I remembered that I wanted to pick up a movie. I'd reserved the film online, and it was waiting for me in one of those grocery-store video-rental boxes. And yes, it was one of those horror movies that I still love.

When I'd reserved the film, I'd imagined myself watching it later that night, alone, on my laptop, scared to death. I don't often do scary movies in a public theater anymore. After more than a decade of teaching and doing youth work in the same town, I'll often run into someone I know as I'm walking out of a horror movie. I'm not up for the conversation that would follow, my position and belief would be impossible to understand, and I don't want to give a bad, or the wrong, impression.

But I wasn't thinking about any of that in that moment. We'd had a great lunch—talking all about life, work, writing, and girls. Then, as we passed the grocery store, I remembered that I was going to pick up that movie...and instinctively blurted out a quick, "Oh, hey, if you don't mind, let me do this one thing quickly." And that was it. I'd left myself open for a moment of criticism.

Now my young and impressionable friend doesn't know about my secret love for horror. "What kind of movie you going to watch?" he asks, seeking only to make small talk. This is not a guy who's riding a wave of conviction. He's not carrying a torch to the outskirts of the city, hoping to chase the monster off the cliff. He's not going to judge me.

But I know that what I watch, read, and listen to does make an impression on those whom I spend time with. My students, my children, my friends...they're all influenced by my choices. And I wonder sometimes if the struggle I face with my love of horror movies isn't primarily an issue of authenticity between God and me. Instead, it's an issue of transparency between me and the people I know. Should I be careful only for myself, or for them, too? Does my renting this film affect my friend's spirituality?

With my friend waiting, I push all the right buttons, grab the movie, and stuff it into the pocket of my jacket. And as we walk toward my car, another verse from Paul rings in my head...

"Blessed are those who do not condemn themselves by what they approve" (Romans 14:22b).

CHAPTER
THE STRUGGLE WITH *SPIRITUAL*
THREE

He's intimate, you know? Like the lover you've always wanted, but never knew you had. He's my best friend, the one who's always been there for me since before I understood what 'having a best friend' meant. He's tangible in the most intangible of ways. I can feel his presence, but I can't see him. It's my time in prayer with him that means the most to me because that's when I feel him showing up most often. Like he is really real. As close to me as you are right now."

I remember sitting there next to Anne on her plaid couch as she spoke about her relationship with God. I was 16 years old, a new Christian. Anne was known in our church for having an unusually deep relationship with God, and I sought her out because that's exactly what I wanted. Her apartment spoke of her profound faith. Books about God and spirituality were all around, dog-eared or laying open to a place she was coming back to. Crosses and other religious images were hung on the stark white walls. Incense was burning atop a bookshelf nearby. Big windows were open so the breeze could come all the way in.

Anne sat across from me with one of those deeply spiritual looks on her face, as if she were smelling the sweetest perfume mixed with spiced bread and coffee. She seemed so deeply connected with The Source that her every word felt deeply meaningful. Quiet, reserved, deeply thoughtful. I wanted what she had—all of it. The nice apartment organized so you could see my relationship with God in the way I set up my world. I wanted that same expression of godliness. Anne's faith was my brass ring, and I was willing to stretch my body as far as I needed in order to grab that prize myself.

"When I first met Jesus, I thought I'd already received everything I needed," Anne confided. "I felt so good and so fulfilled. It felt wonderful. But then a friend told me about the Holy Spirit. And that made me realize I needed more. Jesus wasn't enough, there was one more step. And when the Holy Spirit came in, it was joy on top of joy. It was beyond the feeling I had when I met Jesus, ten times more. And when that happened, I talked in another language."

I'd heard the Pentecostal kids in my high school talk about speaking in tongues before, telling me I didn't really have the Holy Spirit until I'd used them.

In fact, that's what led me to Anne's couch that day. My desire to speak in a language I didn't understand so my belief in God could go deeper. Somehow that would mean I was a real Christian.

We talked more about tongues, and I really wanted them because I truly wanted that deeper relationship with Jesus. And that deeper relationship wasn't the only thing I wanted from Jesus, by the way. I also wanted him to get my parents back together. I wanted a girlfriend. I needed a job, too. So there was a lot on Jesus' plate. But I wanted tongues because I wanted physical confirmation of the change happening in me. Jesus felt real in my heart. I knew something inside was different. Tongues would be the evidence to confirm that change.

"Do you want them?" Anne asked.

And I thought: *Do I really want them?* I really did. "Yes," I said. Convincingly.

We knelt in her living room, and Anne placed her hands on the back of my bowed head. Her hands felt heavy as they rested on what would someday become my bald spot. Anne prayed earnestly.

"Oh, dear Jesus. We love you. I bring to you today my brother Tim, Lord. He's expressed a desire..." Anne's words trailed off in my head, and for a moment I had a keen sense that something different was happening. But then my mind started to wander. Anne had this cool multicolored rug, and with my head bowed, I could see she didn't vacuum very often. There were corn chip crumbs everywhere. Also, Anne must have really liked board games because she kept a lot of them under her sofa. Scrabble and Parcheesi lay under her couch. A small, clear bag of dice. Playing cards.

I struggled to pay attention to our conversation with God. I'd nod and say, "Mmmm, yes Lord," then move my head a bit so I could change my view and look in new places. Did I really want tongues? Why did I want them?

The more Anne prayed, the louder she got. And the louder she got, the more she began to pray in tongues herself. Like I said, this wasn't my first experience with tongues. But hearing Anne pray in tongues right next to me caused a little bit of fear to well up in me. It felt like a combination of several events all happening at once: Like ghosts had entered the room, like my uncle wandered into Christmas dinner in his boxers, like a burning bush, and like a sincere prayer. It was spiritual and uncomfortable and weird all at once.

Then Anne ended her prayer with an "Amen," and that was it. I could tell she was a little disappointed I hadn't spoken in tongues. Honestly, I was too. God didn't show up for me that day. Maybe God was especially busy, looking after starving kids in Africa or working out job details for someone or thinking through weather patterns or attending the ordination of a Catholic priest. I didn't know God's agenda, I just know he wasn't there for me—at least not as I'd hoped.

I felt like God let me down. Anne had this spooky spiritual ability to speak in a language neither of us understood. Why didn't I get it? Maybe I was the problem. Maybe there was no way God was going to give such a special gift to a selfish kid like me, someone who couldn't even pay attention in prayer. Maybe I was too sinful. Anne seemed pretty holy, so my being rotten seemed like a pretty good explanation. Maybe it was a motivation problem...did I want tongues just because the cool Pentecostal kids I was hanging out with had tongues? Was this outward sign of God's presence in me something I needed to confirm God's love? Did I need it to prove that I really was saved, that I really was loved?

I've reflected on that disappointment for a long time. It happened almost 30 years ago, yet it remains a very significant moment in my spiritual journey because it's a time when I sought God with as much passion as I can ever remember having. I'd done my best, you know, letting God know I was in hot pursuit of a deeper connection with him. And nothing happened. I'm sure that says *something* about me and about God. But what?

THE PARADOX OF BEING SPIRITUAL

I think what I wanted that day from both Anne and God was an instant change, as simple as flipping a switch. I didn't want to deepen my walk with God step by step. I wanted immediate transformation.

Don't a lot of us think that way? We want that massive change, but we don't want to participate in the process. For so many years I've wanted spirituality to happen to me—or maybe even in me—but I've not wanted it enough to work for it. I was certainly willing to pray about it. In fact, I'd pray about it with anyone willing to listen to my story about how bad I wanted it. I was willing to read a book or two. And I was open to experiences that would change my perspective about my spirituality or open my eyes to things in me that needed to change. But still, what I wanted to see was dramatic transformation, not gradual progress.

When I was a kid, I remember a commercial for a fitness club where the rock star Cher stood in front of a camera wearing a tank top and shorts that showed off her incredibly fit body. Near the end of the commercial, Cher said, "Face it: If it came in a bottle, everyone would have a great body." I think for much of my life I've been searching for spirituality in a bottle—looking for that book or sermon or belief that will turn me into a Spiritual Hero. But it doesn't work that way—and that's the paradox. I have a deep desire to become the spiritual man I envision, but I seem to lack the dedication to that ideal. I want what I see in the lives of others, but, again and again, it seems I'm unwilling to work for it.

HAVE YOU EVER FELT LET DOWN BY GOD? HOW DID THAT AFFECT YOUR WALK WITH HIM?

I wonder if my longing for a deeper relationship with God, even if I never act on it, makes me more spiritual. Is passion to touch the face of Jesus enough motivation? Does that desire tell the truth of our spirituality? Or, do we need results...does God need to see us do more? Do I need to reach out? Do I need to go to church? Can I live alone in the desert and be spiritual? Can I be spiritual without selling everything I have and giving it all to the poor? I know that my spiritual longing would look different than anyone else's, but what would that look like, exactly? If I grow more spiritual, who will I become? Will I *really* be any different?

Our spirituality begins at that place of desire for God. From God's perspective, our journey begins in his redeeming grace that reaches out to us. But, from our perspective, it's longing. We passionately desire God... to be fixed, to be whole, to find answers, to discover love, to change. Longing is the fuel for making that journey in God. It's in the passion we feel in worship and in the desire we have to sit in God's lap and tell him about our pain and our passion.

WHAT MASSIVE SPIRITUAL CHANGE HAVE YOU BEEN WAITING FOR? ARE YOU PARTICIPATING IN CREATING THAT CHANGE—OR SITTING AROUND WAITING FOR IT TO HAPPEN TO YOU?

But here's the meat of the paradox: We have this passion for a deeper spirituality, and yet, at the same time, we're clueless about how to make it happen. We *want* it, but we don't know how to *be* it. And as we try to figure that out, our spiritual pursuit becomes a journey of appearances. We're not sure how to be spiritual, so we try to *look* spiritual. We think of spirituality as some ideal we need to reach up to, some goal we need to attain. But the reality is that we are already spiritual people. Spirituality is woven into our very souls, our very humanity. I bet if I were to map my spiritual journey and then compare it with a map of my occupational journey, or my journey in relationships, the trajectories would be very similar. Because who I am spiritually is who I am professionally, occupationally, emotionally.

But when we think of spirituality as some goal outside ourselves that we need to attain, we lose the understanding of ourselves as being on our own spiritual journey. We think of spirituality as something to grasp, and when we do grab hold of it, we claim it as ours and want to stay in that "I've found it" place.

There's a big problem with this kind of thinking. We don't always measure up to this spiritual ideal, and the moment we lose sight of the idea that being spiritual is a life journey, that's the moment we begin masking. We paint and polish to try to make ourselves appear more spiritual. We cover up. We change our language. We adopt a life for show. We perform as if we're someone else and desperately hide who we really are.

CURB APPEAL

I have a friend who was trying to sell his house recently, and he was talking about the importance of "curb appeal." When selling a house, you need to dress it up so it looks as good as possible—maybe better than it really is. If you don't have shutters, you add them. If you need coat of paint, you splash one on quickly. You add a few bushes here and there, or you sod the front yard so the place looks better. You find cheap ways to make that old barn look like a new house, so it'll seem attractive to the potential buyer. It's pretty much the same house; you've just made some cheap changes to increase the curb appeal.

When we think of spirituality as some goal we've failed to attain, we're tempted to try to increase the curb appeal of our faith. Because our walk doesn't look like the ideal, we paint the barn. We add in fancy praying. We wear nicer clothes. We spend more time at church. We do stuff to convince others, and maybe ourselves, that there's no question about the quality of the building. We present ourselves as secure and strong spiritual believers.

When we do this, we end up being a lot like the Pharisees Jesus spoke out against. We surround ourselves with things intended to make others think we are more spiritual. Why are we so worried about what other believers think of our spiritual life? Why do we whitewash our walk for others, just so they'll be impressed? Rather than admitting when we're struggling through a dry spiritual time, we often try to mask it by saying all the right things. We mask who we are, create a double life, because we fear people's reactions if we are honest about how we feel about our spiritual selves. Tell someone the truth about your doubt, and you're called "a doubter." Tell a pastor that you're struggling with a sin, and you're labeled. Confide in a friend about a temptation, be honest about a deep emotion, and you're talked about. It's easier to pretend everything is great, because then we can avoid the deeper questions. So we choose the easy road, the one where we look great and use all of the right words.

I have a few spiritual heroes who have attained a spiritual maturity that I truly admire. Their journeys with God seem so even, so balanced and impressive. That's what I want. But as hard as I try (and I have tried), I can't get there. I can't even get close. Okay, so maybe that's because I'm not where they are...I'm not at their life stage, I'm not as old as they are, I don't have that depth, or I have a different kind of depth with God. Maybe I wasn't made to be quiet and re-served all the time. I wasn't made to begin each day with several hours of prayer, seeking God's direction for every problem in my life. I've had to accept that my own spirituality isn't exactly like the folks whose faith I most admire. And, beyond that, I've had to learn that I need to be honest and tell the truth about who I am spiritually. Easy? Not at all. Essential to me becoming who God wants me to be? Absolutely.

UNEARTHING THE SPIRITUAL YOU

Authenticity is rooted in understanding that you can't have someone else's spirituality. We are all spiritually related to one another, but we can't be spiritual clones. If we be-lieve God created each of us to be unique, then we can believe that our spiritual pursuit is also completely unique. Your spirituality is birthed out of your own experience with God and your passion to connect with him. You don't pursue it the way someone pursues a job or a sale at a department store. The spiritual you is discovered as you move through life. You want to know more about your spiritual you? Live more. Laugh more. Pray more. Read more. Search the heart of God more. This is not developed...it is discovered. Unearthing our spiritual person isn't motivated by the phrase, "I want to be." It's moved forward by the words, "I am becoming".

> DO YOU ALLOW HYPOCRISY IN WHEN YOU FEEL INSECURE ABOUT YOUR SPIRITUALITY? HAS THIS CREATED AN ALTERNATE SPIRITUAL IDENTITY IN YOU?

And the journey begins with honesty. I don't know about you, but telling the truth about the spiritual me is difficult. You know, some of the hardest words I've ever had to say are words like, "I've not read my Bible this week," and, "It's been a while since I've prayed." There are times when I gather with other believers and I feel like the most honest thing I could say is, "Now who's this Jesus guy you keep talking about? I feel like I haven't seen him in a long time." Sometimes I feel like I spend more time outside the "Jesus circle" than I spend inside it. I struggle with that because I feel like I should always be able to tell you, chapter and verse, about the quality of my quiet times and the substance of my prayer life. Those aren't things people are typically honest about.

I've met lots of people who have far less biblical knowledge than I do, yet they seem to understand the life of the spirit far more. I've met people whose theology and beliefs were way off, yet they were deeply passionate about knowing the same God I believe in. I've met people the church would be quick to label as hopeless sinners who are way more spiritual than I am. I've been crying out to Jesus for years, and yet, those who haven't appear to be more in touch with him than I am. What does that mean?

Much of what happens to our spiritual lives is unseen. It is truly invisible. Take worship, for example: We may be singing songs and hearing Scripture or whatever, but what's *really* happening in worship at the deepest level can't be seen. Prayer is this way, too. It's difficult to qualify or quantify what's happening. We know *something* is definitely going on. But what? I think what we're able to quantify or explain only scratches the surface.

There's something in me that finds it hard to believe that anything unseen is *really* valuable. Because no one else can see it, it's not serious. But our spiritual selves are extremely important. God is spirit, and if I want to connect with him, the only real way to do that is to connect my spirit with his. If I say that I want to connect with God and don't care about my spiritual side, then I'm lying. If I'm not acting on what I say to be true, then either I don't believe it, or I'm a liar.

So I'm taking steps to build a more active spirituality in my life. What will that look like for me? I don't know. I've have friends who pursue their spirituality so seriously that they take off and spend a weekend at a monastery. Will my spirituality look like that? Will I start fasting, as a way of clearing way the spiritual "fat" that gets in the way of my hearing God? Will I spend hours in prayer?

> IN YOUR QUEST TO BE SPIRITUAL, IS YOUR GOAL TO BE THE PERSON GOD CREATED YOU TO BE—OR TO BE LIKE SOMEONE ELSE?

I'm not sure where my efforts will lead and what spiritual disciplines will work for me. But I want to open myself, to learn to say "yes" to opportunities that deepen my life in the Spirit. In the past, when these kinds of opportunities have come my way, I've tended to be a "no" person. If it wasn't familiar to me, I wasn't interested. I didn't want it. And worse, I didn't feel I needed it. But if I'm going to be that guy who gives himself over to truly being spiritual, then my spirituality has to be ruled by a "holy yes." I need to be open to anything that might help me become more like the person God created me to be. It might be a new worship style. It might be a new way of praying. It might mean journeying into moments when I contemplate the truth found in heresy. It might mean discovering the truth of God in another religion. It does not feel honest to put boundaries on my spiritual journey—and yet, in some ways it feels totally terrifying.

WHAT ASPECTS OF YOUR SPIRITUALITY ARE YOU HIDING FROM OTHERS?

We may journey through deserted places and times when we feel spiritually lost and alone. In the past I've thought of those desert times as a curse, or possibly a message from God about how I've strayed. But I don't think that's the best way to think about those times. Every journey, no matter how great or rotten it is, goes through these places. It can't always be butterflies and roses...both experiences are important. Both tell the honest truth of who we are. And we will feel a conflict of depth...times when we feel as spiritually shallow as if we're living in a half an inch of water, as well as times when we're as deep as an ocean. Neither tells the whole truth about who we are, spiritually. We need to embrace both.

We have to rise higher than slogan spirituality. Can we love God beyond the bumper sticker theology that has taken over today's Christianity? Popular slogans like *HIS PAIN, YOUR GAIN* and *BOUGHT WITH A PRICE* and *WWJD?* and all those others probably have a ton of theological truth in them, but the moment they started printing them on T-shirts was the exact moment a lot of us stopped really thinking about their meaning. At that point, those words left the realm of spiritual pursuit and entered the market of Christian consumerism, where even the most profound theological truths are for sale—sometimes at a discount.

Imagine that…you're able to own the truth about the life of Jesus for cheap. But I don't want a faith that can be summed up on a T-shirt.

What I think I do want, what I think we all need, is a strong first step. We need to admit—to ourselves and others—that spirituality is a struggle. But we can't stop there. We need a starting place from which we can move forward. What if we stopped taking the great gift of our spirituality for granted? What if we took on our spiritual journey as our most important pursuit ever? What if we realized that our spiritual selves need cultivation—they need to be fed differently, exercised differently, and exposed to different things.

We need to live every day recognizing that our spiritual lives need care and attention. We need to take on spiritual mentors who will challenge us, who won't let us skate by, who will ask us those tough questions we hate to answer and say those difficult things we don't want to hear.

And we need to expose ourselves to those things that will make us stretch, force us to reexamine our beliefs, and move us upward toward a different spiritual place. Maybe this is through prayer. Maybe we do this by finding people with whom we can be honest about where we are spiritually. But I think we need to allow these deepest parts of us out of hiding, so they can breathe and grow.

A KITCHEN-FLOOR DISCOVERY

Recently my son and I were trying to pray together. Well, I was trying to pray. Jake was just being seven.

We were lying on the kitchen floor of our church. We'd been given a workbook full of Scripture verses and prayer starters to read through and pray through.

WHAT IS THE NEXT SPIRITUAL STEP FOR YOU? WHAT CAN YOU DO RIGHT NOW TO BEGIN DEVELOPING A DEEPER SPIRITUALITY?

But I was struggling with that task. Jake wanted to talk, and I wanted to talk to him. As you might guess by now, I'm not a huge fan of long, extended prayer times. My mind wanders. I start to daydream. I suspect that Jake struggles in the same way. But we were plugging away—me trying to set a good spiritual example, and Jake being my mini-me nemesis.

Before we even opened the workbook, I encouraged Jake to think about the people he loves, and we would pray for them. So we prayed—first for our immediate family, and then for pretty much everyone else he could think of. We named a lot of people, and we prayed quickly. I think we prayed for everyone Jake has ever met in less than ten minutes.

Then, after the speed-prayer was over, we moved on to the workbook. We were reading Scriptures and praying through the various topics—and Jake kept asking questions about everything. Could he write in the book here or there? What did that word mean? Would it be okay if he read the Scriptures? (Which he did, guessing at words he didn't know and giving the verses brand new interpretations!)

It was exhausting. After a while, I wasn't into the experience at all—but to be honest, I wasn't very into it from the very start.

Near the end of the workbook, we came to a place that asked us to read a passage of Scripture and then draw a picture of God we could relate to, an image that made God understandable to us. I tried reading the passage to Jake, but I could tell he wasn't interested. He wasn't getting anything from those words. But we pushed on. I read the passage aloud a few times, read the explanation again, and then turned the paper sideways, so both he and I could have a little bit of room to draw.

I don't remember what I drew. I was focusing on drawing something from the Scripture—I don't recall what it was. When I looked over at Jake's side of the sheet, he had drawn the sickliest looking God—skinny, with a poorly shaped head, a smile, and a frail little stick body...but with these two huge hands. Large. Ginormous. Hands big enough to handle just about anything happening in the world, in my life, or in the life of my seven-year-old son. "See, Dad?" Jake said. "God has huge hands."

WHEN HAVE YOU HEARD GOD SPEAK INTO YOUR LIFE?

And I believed him. That week, I'd not been feeling spiritual at all, and I'd felt even less spiritual on the floor of the church kitchen. I was carrying the burden of our family finances. I was struggling over the content of this book. I was hurting over a friend who was sick. I was carrying a lot, trying to carry it all myself while not letting Jake see how weighed down I was.

Did Jake know all that? I bet he didn't. Did God know? I believe he did. Did God inspire Jake to draw that picture, to remind me that I didn't have to carry it all myself? I realized in that moment that God is still God. And when I'm honestly seeking him even in the midst of circling the spiritual drain, he speaks through the drawing of a seven-year-old kid.

CHAPTER
FOUR

UNBOXING GOD

I never dated in college. Not really. I don't think I was too ugly to date: I definitely saw people hooking up who were no better looking than I was. I don't think I was particularly gross or uninteresting. But I *was* socially awkward. I never really knew what to say in public. Like when a group of us would be sitting at the dinner table, talking about whatever professor was particularly funny or ridiculously difficult that day. I was the guy at the end of the table thinking, "Yeah, I had him today, too...that's hysterical!"—but on the outside I was a total poker face. Or I looked angry. I was introverted beyond introverted. Deeply socially inept. At least, I felt that way—still do. And that didn't make me the kind of guy the girls sought after. I was, in a word, *undatable*.

So on those Friday nights, when everyone else was out having fun (at least I imagined they were all having fun), I found things to do that would hide my lone wolf status. Often, I went to the library.

I didn't really enjoy reading that much, but I loved being around books. I liked book titles. I liked the clear plastic covers they used to put around books. I liked sitting on one of those roller stools they kept in the library aisles and looking up at the books towering over me. I loved being surrounded by all that information. I imagined what it would be like if all those writers were in that room looking down on me and telling me about their books. What might they say? Would they take turns? Would they talk over one another? Would they have vigorous academic debates? Or would they tell me to get out of the library and find a girlfriend?

My favorite aisle had the bound copies of the apocrypha, the pseudepigrapha, and other ancient religious writings that weren't included in the biblical canon for one reason or another. These books often had weird names. Some of them are clearly fakes. Others are named after famous ancient people, but clearly weren't written by those people. Some include different versions of stories and ideas that appear in the Bible. Others feature ideas that aren't consistent with orthodox Christianity.

I found these books fascinating. Although some of the books were printed recently, the stories themselves were old—they *felt* old. Reading them felt mysterious, almost dirty. There I was at an evangelical Christian college reading stuff that said to me, "Maybe the truth you've learned from the Bible and your religion classes isn't all that's true."

I loved the way those stories made my head feel bigger. Not smarter but *larger*, in the sense that I was learning more about The Book that so many of my friends thought of as beginning with Genesis and ending with Revelation. I fell in love with the "what ifs" that surrounded these stories. What if there's more to our story than is found in the accepted canon of Scripture? What if Jesus did all kinds of important stuff that's not mentioned in the four gospels? What if there were lots of other Christian writers and apostles whose thinking was just as important as Paul's? What did they say? Why are books like First and Second Maccabees included in the Catholic Bible, but not mine? Is it possible those books are as authoritative as Exodus? Why don't we read Clement of Alexandria and consider that God was moving his hand too? Was it just because some group of men met and decided these other writings didn't fit? Or because God directed these writings out of authoritative Scripture?

WHAT WOULD HAPPEN TO YOUR SPIRITUAL JOURNEY IF YOU SPENT ONE WEEK STUDYING A DOCUMENT ABOUT JESUS WRITTEN IN THE SAME TIME AS ONE OF THE GOSPELS?

There's a marriage that happens when each of us becomes a believer in Jesus. The love relationship begins when God starts pursuing us, and the vows are Scripture. We, as believers, keep these vows inviolate, which means we do not break them. We uphold them as the substance of our agreement with God, and we tell God we love him and believe what's been written down for us in his Word. But there's a phrase that we often add to those vows, something we believe, but never say aloud: That the Bible is all there is to know about God, that everything that comes along before or after it is a fib.

But the Bible never claims it contains all there is to know. In fact, the very last verse of John's Gospel says, "Jesus did many other things as well. If every one of them were written down, I suppose that even the whole world would not have room for the books that would be written" (John 21:25). I realized that I had defined Scripture as closed, even though Scripture never claims that it's closed. And, honestly, I think I wanted to believe the Bible was a closed book because it matched my belief that God was a known quantity. Those were the two bookends of my neatly pieced together spiritual world.

But those books that stared back at me as I sat on the floor of the college library opened a new world of questions in me. Is there more we can know about God? What if there are stories in these other books that really get it right? I understood these questions not as temptations planted there by Satan's scheming. Instead, I understood this as a moment of educational clarity. I was paying thousands of dollars to get PhDs to make me think, and there in the library, I actually was thinking.

But this chapter isn't about whether or not the biblical canon should include other writings. And it's not about whether one or two things in these other writings are correct. My question is bigger than that. What if what we've been told about God, his Word, his existence, is just the beginning? What if we've mis-understood some of the truth God wants us to hear? What if he's bigger than we've thought? What if he's broader than what we've understood him to be?

THE DISCOVERY OF THE UNBOXED GOD

HOW HAVE YOU LIMITED GOD BY THE WAY YOU'VE DEFINED HIM? WHAT WOULD HAPPEN IN YOUR WALK IF YOU SPENT ONE DAY CONTEMPLATING THE LIMITLESSNESS OF GOD?

I once had a conversation with a guy who didn't want his daughter dating someone from another race. We sat in his office, and he told me all the reasons why he felt it wasn't right for his daughter (who was white) to date a black guy. He talked about the "crazy-looking babies" they'd have (his perspective, not mine), the societal back-lash they'd face, and on and on. But the kicker of the entire conversation was when he pointed to the very traditional portrait of Jesus he had on his wall and said, "I want my daughter to date someone who looks like this...like Jesus."

It took a while for me to unpack that with him. Did he believe Jesus was white with brown hair and a nicely trimmed beard, like the one in the picture? Yeah. Did he mean he wanted his kid to mar-ry someone with blue eyes and a peaceful look? Yes, again. Turns out, this guy was convinced Jesus was a white American, with hair that was perfectly combed and his face always clean.

As much as that frustrated me, I realize I've done that same thing to God many times. I've believed the portrait that's been painted for me. I've trusted the picture of Jesus that I've been handed from tradition and from the churches I've attended. I've accepted that what I've been handed is the truth, the whole truth, and nothing but the truth. I've not trusted my belief enough to dig through it the way a child digs through a sandbox searching for their lost toys.

But Jesus is not the picture that was hanging on this guy's wall. Jesus was from the Mid East—not the Midwest. He surely didn't have blue eyes. He likely did not have great looking hair. He was, in all likelihood, a swarthy, sunburned, dirty-haired guy who looked at home among the rough-edged fishermen who surrounded him. His hands would have had splinter marks. His face would have had big bites on it. He would have smelled. There's no way we'd want to sit next to him at the church potluck.

In fact, if this guy's daughter brought home a guy who looked just like Jesus, I'm not sure he'd be too happy.

But that's not the point.

It's not just that we trust in these portraits of Jesus that are wrong. We believe silly and unbiblical stuff about the character and nature of God. We trust traditional views that aren't always based on Scripture. We trust tales that are not accurate.

But that's not the point, either.

When it comes to what we've heard about God—whether it's about his grace and love, or his judgment, or what heaven is like, or what we have to do to be in right relationship with him—we somehow believe not only that these things are true, but that they are the end of the discussion. Ask someone what heaven will be like, and you'll get the answer—streets of gold, angels, and God's throne. We think we've got it all figured out.

But as I reflect back on that conversation with the guy worried about who was dating his daughter and consider the wonder created in me those nights sitting in the library, I understand there's more. There's more to heaven than we'll ever understand in this world. There's more to the nature, character, and goodness of God than we'll ever know in our human bodies. There's more to the story of Jesus...more that he did, more that he said, more people he healed...than we can know right now.

WHAT COULD HAPPEN IF YOU ASKED "WHY?" ABOUT EVERY ONE OF YOUR BELIEFS?

And the frustrating thing is that, even though I've acknowledged these mysteries, I've tended to wrap them up in a box and put them on a shelf for discovery at another time in my life. I've mentally set them aside, imagining that they bore no weight on my life in God right now. They were reserved for exploration later on in my life, or they were roped off as inappropriate because they led me into worlds of ideas that were patently unbiblical.

But when your life in God doesn't include ongoing discovery, you'll soon find yourself hitting dead ends in your spiritual journey. When there's no possibility of discovery to challenge you forward, you end up going nowhere. What can you uncover when you already know everything? What more can you learn about God if you feel you've already discovered all of it in Sunday school or heard everything you need to know from the 1,000 sermons you've sat through? I've often felt like I was moving forward in God when I was actually just retracing my steps. Like those times when I've relearned an old truth or rediscovered something about God I had known for a long time while talking with a friend. I've felt like I was growing, but really all I had been doing was rehashing stuff I already knew. There was no discipleship or mentoring to move me forward. It was just the same old stuff that I'd already known for years.

WHAT IS IT YOU WOULD MOST LIKE TO LEARN ABOUT GOD? WHAT DO YOU MOST WANT TO DISCOVER?

Certainly, authentic spirituality involves more than just memorizing what has been written down or rehashing what we already know; it also means delving into stuff we'd never known. It means uncovering ideas we didn't know existed, and it means considering thinking that lies outside what is "acceptable" and what most of us typically study. It means being willing to engage and argue with new thoughts. It means digging through those ancient manuscripts we've been told are untrue. It means asking crazy philosophical questions about God, discovering theologies we've never considered before, and considering alternate ideas that might be as right as our own. And it means committing to live this way for our entire lives, not just for the next week.

What kind of people would we become if our lives were marked by a constant, unending, and uncontrollable desire to know all that we can know of God? The road that leads out of a dead-end spirituality is a road we often must create ourselves. We do that through a willingness to explore, to think deeply, and to reconsider and test our own beliefs.

You know the phrase, "Don't put God in a box"? I think we end up doing that much more than we realize. At first, we use theological words, philosophical ideas, and denominational beliefs in a genuine effort to understand more about the God we love. But too often we let those words define God's limits more than they describe his limitlessness. We start to imagine that we've got God all figured out, that we know exactly how God works—and how God would never work. We believe God has already revealed to us everything we need to know, and the rest we have to blindly accept by faith.

The Living God cries from eternity to be released from the boxes we've built around him. God wants to be discovered, to be learned about, to be imagined, to be dreamt about. Are there places we dare not go, ones that might lead us into dangerous territory? Certainly. But God wants us to know him better. The invitation to experience God more deeply isn't an invitation that comes from me. It's God's invitation to you. As the psalmist says, "Taste and see that the Lord is good" (Psalm 34:8). God invites you to move into him, push around and discover him, try him over and over. His goodness is not experienced in just one bite, it's discovered over a lifetime of continued tasting.

I think God longs for us to us to open the box, to pull back the curtain. This means realizing that the fuzzy, smoke-filled images we've seen for so long are just hazy reflections of something so very real, more real than we could possibly imagine. Pulling back that curtain means asking ourselves what and who God really is. Where could he have come from? What else can we know of his true nature? How have we limited him?

Let's commit to turning off the smoke machines so that we can more clearly see the real character of our Heavenly Father. Let's adopt an attitude of discovery about who God is. Let's adopt this same attitude about the Scripture we read and the songs we sing. Let's scrutinize the sermons we hear and question whether they seek to wrap God up more tightly or open him to greater discovery. Let's evaluate every Bible study and every devotional, asking if they lead us into the mysterious or tell us things we already know. Let's dig deep, allowing God to become unboxed in us.

ARE THERE BELIEFS THAT YOU'VE ADOPTED WITHOUT REALLY UNDERSTANDING THEM? HOW MUCH OF YOUR OWN FAITH DO YOU REALLY OWN?

MOORINGS

Of course, we can't do this whole unboxing thing without admitting that our thinking can easily get distorted. Left completely unchecked and on their own, our minds can do really nutty things. You don't need me to tell you this...look around at the freakish cults who draw inspiration from their own particular distorted views of certain Scriptures. Check out all the "end times people" who overly love Revelation. There are more than enough examples of people whose search for new truth has clouded their understanding of who God is.

So even as I'm telling you to question and search through all you've been taught about God, I want to remind you to root yourself in the deepest truths of who God is. There are some things about God we just know, like we know the layout of our bedroom without the lights on. There are some truths about God that can anchor us, some foundations to which we can moor ourselves in this discovery. That God is Love. That he is Truth, and would never lead us astray. That the Scriptures have given us a picture of his character and his nature. And that God's nature was revealed to us in Jesus, his son. So when we have questions about what God is like, we don't need to start from scratch. There is no question that God has revealed himself to us in Scripture. Whether we know everything about him or not is open for more discovery.

Authenticity leads us back to Scripture. It allows us to ask those great questions of discovery and allows us to test our answers against what Scripture has taught us. But that means we have to know what the Bible says. We have to know the ins and outs of Scripture. We have to know the cultural context that shapes the Old Testament. We have to know the questions the early church struggled with. We have to understand why, for example, the question of eating meat that had been sacrificed to idols was such a huge question for the audience to whom Paul was writing. We have to know the important cities of the Old and New Testaments. Scripture is both the launching point for our discovery and the port to which we return.

Too often, I think, we view Scripture the same way some of us look at our favorite lake. We might look at the surface and see the ripples, the reflection of the sunlight, the tiny little bubbles floating up here, and think we're seeing the lake. But the reality is that there's so much more—an entire ecosystem under the surface. In the same way, we might read a minor prophet's verbal onslaught against religious leaders or Paul's urging women to be silent in church—and we think we're seeing all we need to see. But we're wrong. We have to research the stuff under the surface. We can't skim along the top of the water and imagine we know all there is to know. Our commitment to dig beyond the surface of Scripture is in no way a thumbing of our noses at the clear message of Scripture. Instead, it's a desire to know God and his Word for us even more intimately.

We also need people in our lives who are committed to go on the journey of discovery with us. Smart people don't explore alone. Lewis had Clark, Columbus had at least three ships. Like them, we need other people who are committed to engage in this journey of exploration with us. We need other travelers who are discovering stuff on their own and coming back to us to share what they are learning, just as we share where God is leading us. We need a community that keeps us grounded, helping us sort through where we are wrong and where tradition is wrong. We need these people to remind us that our human reasoning, just like all human reasoning, is flawed and in need of constant vetting.

THINK ABOUT THE LAST BIBLE PASSAGE YOU MEMORIZED. HAVE YOU CONSIDERED THE CULTURAL AND POLITICAL TIME IN WHICH THE PASSAGE WAS WRITTEN? DO YOU KNOW THE PASSAGE JUST WELL ENOUGH TO REPEAT IT, OR HAVE YOU FULLY UNDERSTOOD IT AND MADE IT YOUR OWN?

I'm thankful to have people like that in my life. I'm grateful for people who are serious about thinking and rethinking what they believe to be true about God and who aren't too concerned about stepping on toes. I've got friends like that...do you? They include both Christians and nonChristians, people I love who don't mind kicking around the theological dirt with me, considering the *what ifs* and *how dids* about God. Despite both my education and calling, at first I was terrified of having such conversations. What would people think if I asked questions about my own core beliefs? Was I willing to admit that some of them knew more about theology than I did? Would I have the courage to tell them I felt they were wrong, and would they be confused if I continued to love them even if we disagreed? What if they chose not to believe that God is real or that God loves them? What if I began to doubt my own belief in God?

Is it really possible for us to maintain our love for God and the body of Christ while still questioning some of what we've understood to be true for so long? Could we really hold one another in check without feeling guilty for asking questions about tradition and certainty? Oddly enough, I think having these concerns and sharing them with one another helps to keep us from getting too far off base. Maybe it's the Holy Spirit that reminds us that caution is both necessary and healthy as we seek to discover more about God and our faith. But caution should never be an excuse to stop asking questions or considering new ideas.

LOOSENING THE CHAINS

I think we have to hold our own personal theologies very loosely. We should seek to walk ever closer to God, while admitting we don't have it all figured out. We cling to the God who is the source of all truth, even as we loosen our grip on the certainties of our own theology.

Now maybe you've never even thought about the fact that you have a theology. Perhaps you think theology is only for pastors and seminary professors. But *you* have a theology, a group of beliefs about God that you've decided are true. Theology is something all of us have, whether we talk overtly about these beliefs or not. All of us have opinions and thoughts about spiritual things. And authenticity demands that we hold those beliefs loosely. We allow them to be questioned, to be prodded at, to be shoved around. The question shouldn't be, "How can I protect what I believe from being questioned?" or even, "How can I best defend my beliefs?" Instead we should be looking at questions like, "What is the best way to open my beliefs so they can grow?" and, "Who are the safe people who can challenge me to a deeper faith?"

This process of theological discovery may involve unlearning some of what we've always taken for granted, some of the stuff our churches, families, and traditions have taught us that we've never thought through for ourselves. We may need to let go some of the stuff we've "always known," to make room for the new truths God wants us to know about him. Can we hold onto our foundational beliefs even as we learn the new? Yes. But do we need to cling to everything we've ever been told? No, and a group of wise fellow travelers can provide a safe place for us to sort all that out.

WHAT ARE SOME ESSENTIAL ELEMENTS IN YOUR THEOLOGY? HAVE YOU ALLOWED YOUR THEOLOGY TO BE CHALLENGED AND SHAPED BY PEOPLE WISER THAN YOU?

This entire process—the searching through Scriptures, the exploration of our beliefs, and the willingness to loosen our grip on what we already "know"—needs to be guided and moved along by God's Holy Spirit. Unless the Spirit is in this process with us, our commitment to understand God authentically isn't anything more than a philosophical or intellectual project. Unless the Spirit is guiding us, all we will gather is the typical surface stuff—the same things we have always learned. But with God's Spirit in us and with us, I believe we are guaranteed an unending discovery of new truth, which leads to an even deeper understanding of the God who is Truth. With his Holy Spirit in the journey with us, God is unboxed, discovered anew, loved deeper and more authentically. It becomes a journey of discovery that we own.

I feel like my own process of unboxing God began early in my life, much earlier than I'd have expected. It actually occurred before I became a Christian—and in a way that I believe is pretty untypical.

It happened when I was about 15 years old. I sleeping at my dad's house in a bed near a large bay window. In the middle of the night I had a dream about Jesus—which was weird because I'd never really thought too much about Jesus up to that point in my life. The Jesus I dreamt about wasn't like the one that guy hoped would date his daughter. This Jesus had huge brown eyes. So big and expressive that they looked almost like two huge opened plastic containers of chocolate pudding. Every other feature on this dream-Jesus was normal, but his eyes were unlike anything I'd ever seen. And I remember looking into those eyes and asking questions: "Are you really real?" and, "Do you really love me? Really?" Jesus didn't answer my questions with his voice; he never moved his mouth. But I knew the answer because I could see it in his eyes. Somewhere, deep in the creaminess of a chocolate so vivid you could have scooped a little out with your finger, Jesus was answering: *Yes, I do love you. Yes, I am real—really.* I knew, in that moment, beyond any doubt, that Jesus is every bit as real as I am, as real as I can imagine and far beyond that. I remember looking deeply into those deep brown eyes and feeling something powerful...the warm welcome of my Heavenly Father. Acceptance. God's openness to who I am and his unconditional love for me.

HOW HAVE YOU BEEN KEEPING GOD IN A CAGE?

I realize that's not a typical dream—and that you might think I sound a little crazy. But I think of that dream as more than just a moment where God revealed something to me about the nature of his son. I see that dream as a moment when God gave me permission to seek him. A moment in which God reminded me that he is always eager to be found, and not just within the rigid lines of orthodoxy.

I know my dream is unusual. It does not follow tradition, it does not make me sound sane, it is not normal. But if our God can shape the world with his hands, can call forth life with his voice, why can't he use a dream to lead us toward him? And while that dream is certainly not my only basis for understanding who God is, it's an image I rely on when I think about how God feels about me, and it's my starting point for dreaming about the God I love so much, the God who is far too big to ever be contained in the cages we create for him.

CHAPTER
EVANGELISTICALLY CHALLENGED
FIVE

Sitting in my car at the downtown stoplight, it was tough to make out his exact words. But I knew the guy on the corner was saying something he thought was important. So I decided to roll the window down a crack and listen.

Well, actually, he wasn't "saying" anything—he was shouting. And he sounded furious. Dressed in a suit that, to be honest, was a little too small for him, he looked…uncomfortable. Was that why he sounded so angry?

He wasn't talking to anyone in particular. He was talking to all of us—his street corner congregation. We'd been called together in that moment by divine appointment, I guess, to hear that we were all doomed. We were going to "Heeeeellllll," and apparently we needed the "Salvayshun of Jeasoush."

The more I listened to the man, the angrier I got. "Is that my God he's talking about?" I thought to myself. If so, why does the Jesus he's talking about feel so foreign to me? Why is he using such a hateful tone to talk about God's great love? And why is his street corner sermon making *me* so angry?

I needed a respite from his bantering. I flicked the radio on and Bon Jovi's "You Give Love a Bad Name" flowed from my speakers. It felt like a song straight from God's mouth to my heart. No, that song doesn't have anything to do with evangelism or this sweaty preacher in his too-small suit. And yet, in a way, it spoke right back to him.

Love is not proclaimed as much as it is lived. Love is not angry, and it does not exist so we can twist it into something else or use it for profit. If that's what we're doing, it may be persuasive, and it may be passionate, but it's not love.

And that's the truth I felt like that man needed to hear. I imagined him going home and thinking about what a good job he'd done that day. I suspected that later that night he'd sit down with the pocket knife his grandpap had given him and cut a few notches in the binding of his Bible for the souls he'd saved that day. And I figured that he'd assume any negative comments he heard were simply a case of his being "persecuted for Christ"—never suspecting his own anger and intolerance were provoking the angry comments.

So I did what any self-respecting person would do in that situation. I rolled my window all the way down. I turned my classic rock radio station up as loud as it would go, and I stared back at the man—hoping he'd hear God's great prophet from New Jersey, Jon Bon Jovi, and the truth he was declaring in that song. And if that angry preacher man didn't hear it, maybe the people passing by would hear it and would know there's another way. Maybe they'd understand that this guy's message, even if his words contained some truth, was being said in a way that didn't communicate God's heart. Did God place me on that street corner at that moment so I could offer truth from a sinner to balance these lies from the mouth of a saint?

> WHAT'S THE BEST WAY TO SHARE JESUS WITH SOMEONE? DO WE HAVE TO USE WORDS? IS LIVING FOR HIM ENOUGH?

SHARING THE GOSPEL

Could it be that "Proclamation Truth"—a gospel that's screamed in a way that makes it sound like a dead-end road—doesn't work the way we Christians want it to work? Like, when a preacher gets up and starts to tell you how faith is the beginning of all your happiness, but as he describes what that means, it sounds more like the end of your fun. Or, those evangelists who declare truth so definitively, talking about all the reasons why what they believe is the only right way to grasp Jesus. Where they talk with absolute authority about Jesus' views on stuff Jesus never said anything about, and yet they know, by the power of the Holy Spirit and their own inspired study, that they are right beyond all right. Divinely correct, in an untouchable way.

Sometimes I think God must really hate evangelism. Maybe he looks at us with all of our Four Spiritual Laws booklets and wishes we'd put down the tracts and just live lovingly for him.

STOP AND THINK ABOUT THE WAY JESUS "DID EVANGELISM." HOW DID HE DO IT? WHAT CAN WE LEARN FROM HIM?

I know there was a time when street preaching was an important part of American church culture. More recently, there was a time when walking the sidewalks passing out tracts that told "the truth about Jesus" was an essential part of most every youth ministry. I understand that the predominant framework in which we've tended to understand evangelism has involved going out and sharing the gospel with strangers we'd never see again. I get that this is what evangelism has meant for many of us. But I have to ask…is this right? Does it make sense? And does it reflect God's heart for the lost?

I know the Old Testament prophets spent a lot of time warning people of God's immanent judgment. And the New Testament includes stories of Peter and Paul addressing large groups and sharing the truth about God. This concept of evangelism shaped American Christianity. Who were the Christians? They were the warners…ready to remind you that you're headed to hell, that you needed to turn or burn. Truth was not something to be discussed, it was to be accepted. Decisions were not gradual, they were immediate. God was not a gentleman, waiting for and walking with people who loved him, he was more like a construction guy with a sledgehammer. Truth was delivered like a shovel to the face, and so was God's love.

This is who we've been—or at least part of who we've been. And that's why I have to ask: Is it okay to love God yet hate the way "evangelism" is often done? Is it okay that I'm not eager to force feed my beliefs to people before I've learned their names? Will I end up with less stuff in heaven, living in a closet while everyone else is walking around in God's presence? Does Jesus really want all of us to be out there every day telling the whole freaking world about our faith?

It's an important question. I know there are Christians who feel it's our duty as believers to talk openly about our faith all the time. They sincerely believe faithfulness to God is measured by one thing: The number of people we've prayed with to receive Christ.

Just today I spoke with someone about a Christian camp she'd been to. I said, "Tell me about your camp. What did you do?" Her response was to tell me the number of students who'd maked a first-time commitment to Christ. I told her that was great and then probed further, asking for more info about the time at camp. Again, I got salvation statistics. I never really got any other information. From her perspective, a Christian camp was only about getting kids saved. What about discipleship? Fun? Dealing with deep hurts? Gaining confidence? Scripture memory? Is the only measure of Christian success (whatever that is) the number of people who give in to our pitch?

Now I have to admit, I feel great when I'm able to convince someone I'm right about God. And my face sinks a bit when I hear someone else's incredible evangelism story and don't have a similar story to share. It's easy for us to feel good about both our salvation and our status in God's eyes (and in other believers' eyes as well) when we've spent time sharing God's truth with someone, and then that person tumbles into faith due to our skilled technique, our powerful repetition of memorized Scriptures, and our general charm.

WHICH IS IT FOR YOU:
"EVANGELISM =
WINNING AN
ARGUMENT" OR
"EVANGELISM =
TELLING YOUR STORY"?
WHICH DO YOU THINK
IS MOST EFFECTIVE
IN HELPING OTHERS
ENCOUNTER CHRIST?

But I think "faith in God" and "debate" have been inappropriately wed together for far too long. When it comes to evangelism, we've done the argument thing, hoping people will be convinced by our reasoning or just give in to our persistence. We've made attempts to use science to prove faith, and we've used faith to try to prove science. We've asked effective questions (If you died tonight...). We've used every sort of media. We've walked all the roads...the catchy, the kitschy, the weird. And we've often done things so very counter to our own comfort, abilities, and passions, all in hopes that people would cross the fence into our Jesus Camp. We've even put plastic fish on our cars. What the heck is that all about?

I know this struggle firsthand. I once kissed a baby pig while sharing the gospel with two young women. It was a hot day, and maybe the sun was getting to me. But I wanted these women to feel I was interested in their lives. I was trying to be someone else, someone not me. I wanted to show that I was concerned about the poverty in their community, the way people were living, and their food supply. The woman showed me her pig, which had a large tumor. My heart broke for this hungry woman, so I kissed it (the pig, not its tumor). But I don't even like pigs. I wasn't all that moved that her pig had a tumor. I kissed the pig because I wanted this woman to hear what I had to say. I wanted her to be open to letting the gospel change her life. If kissing a pig might make that happen, I was willing to pucker.

I've listened to a lot of evangelism stories and led students on outings where they were supposed to share the gospel. After reflecting on those events and listening to the tales, I've decided our evangelism is all too often done for the purpose of making us feel better about ourselves. We want to do something for Jesus—we *need* to do something for Jesus—and, well, evangelism is one right thing to do. We do evangelism because we feel we're supposed to, and youth workers like me plan evangelism events because they seem like cool programs for their kids. But I tend to hear a lot of "me" in evangelism stories. I hear the struggle for success in them. And I hear the implication that God's acceptance of us hinges on the success of our evangelistic efforts.

Maybe that focus on success comes partly from an expectation that our own attempts at evangelism will get the kind of reactions we see in Scriptures. I want my evangelism story to include moments like this one, when Peter was at the Beautiful Gate and took that opportunity to evangelize a lame man who was begging for money:

> Then Peter said, "Silver or gold I do not have, but what I do have I give you. In the

name of Jesus Christ of Nazareth, walk." Taking him by the right hand, he helped him up, and instantly the man's feet and ankles became strong. He jumped to his feet and began to walk. Then he went with them into the temple courts, walking and jumping, and praising God. When all the people saw him walking and praising God, they recognized him as the same man who used to sit begging at the temple gate called Beautiful, and they were filled with wonder and amazement at what had happened to him. (Acts 3:6-10)

I want results. I want some dude in a wheelchair to start walking after I share the gospel. I want to see 50 people accept Jesus when I offer my testimony.

But that's not my experience—and it creates instant guilt. Why don't I always have the right words to say? Am I not filled enough with God's spirit? Why don't I notice people at the gate, hungry and needing healing? Do I lack the focus God expects from me? Why can't I heal people? We see so much power in the New Testament, and yet so little power in our own lives and in our own evangelism. We hear Bible stories like where the leper gets healed, or the woman stops bleeding, or the kid awakens from his death-sleep. We believe that's what Jesus expects of us, and when our lives aren't flooded with those kinds of experiences, we feel guilty. So we're tempted to make the one student salvation the story of our camp. Or we stand on a street corner pouring our hearts out, claiming those lost souls for heaven or accepting the angry responses as persecution (which makes God love us more).

Somewhere along the way we've lost the whole point. We've come to believe that evangelism isn't about the person we're talking to; evangelism is somehow about us. It's about how convincing we can be. It's about how many people we "get" for Jesus. It's about us doing a good job. It's about our efforts, our plans, our stories, and our successes. And maybe that's why there's so much emotion tied to our evangelism. It's not primarily because we're so excited about someone coming into God's kingdom. Sure, we're pleased about that. But the *real* excitement is that we got the win. It's not so much about changing someone else's eternal story as it as about adding to our own story, enhancing our Christian credibility, and gaining brownie points in Godland. Jesus gets the credit, but only after we tell the emotion of the moment, the study we did, the words we used, the rebuttals we faced, and the joy we felt. Winning one of these "You need Jesus" sidewalk showdowns makes us feel so smart. Who doesn't love besting an opponent?

But what if we lose one of those arguments? Does that means God's logic has lost? Or are we just guilty because we've failed to be convincing enough?

THE TEXTURE OF AUTHENTIC EVANGELISM

Now I'm not denying that Jesus instructs believers to tell other people about their faith. And the Scriptures urge us to be ready to defend our faith. As it says 1

Peter 3:15: "Always be prepared to give an answer to everyone who asks you to give the reason for the hope that you have." But sometimes we forget the next line of that same verse: "But do this with gentleness and respect."

How do we do that? How do we share faith in Christ—the reason for our hope—with gentleness and respect? How do we "do evangelism" with honesty, with authenticity, with integrity, with love?

WHAT IS THE VALUE OF DISCUSSING TRUTH INSTEAD OF PROCLAIMING IT?

The shape and texture of authentic evangelism needs to be about searching and talking together. And part of this is a commitment to being transparent about deep issues and honest about real questions. We've grown very comfortable with keeping our true selves locked away. Because of that, we find it much easier to think of evangelism as if it's about being prepared to speak to a "stranger," when, really, evangelism ought to be about sharing our lives and talking about what matters most. It ought to be honest conversation. It ought to be about transparency.

And transparency is terrifying. Really telling someone about Jesus means speaking honestly about my walk with God. It means sharing the faith I have, not the faith I *wish* I had. It means admitting that there are issues I know nothing about, and learning from that other person things I need to know. It means sharing my own journey as a way of helping others in their journeys, not offering proofs to make a decision upon. It means looking for God's truth together.

You know, there's a passage from the final chapter of Matthew's gospel that's often cited as the reason we do evangelism. Near the very end of his time with the disciples, Jesus says these words—words that have become known as the Great Commission:

> Then Jesus came to them and said, "All authority in heaven and on earth has been given to me. Therefore go and make disciples of all nations, baptizing them in the name of the Father and of the Son and of the Holy Spirit, and teaching them to obey everything I have commanded you. And surely I am with you always, to the very end of the age." (Matthew 28:18-20)

How do we hear that passage? Do we hear Jesus' call to "go and make disciples" as a command to leave our current lives behind and head off to evangelize people on the other side of the world? Is it all about going to new places, finding people we've never met, and telling them about Jesus? I think that's what most of us hear—and that may surely be God's calling for some of us. In English that "go" certainly reads like a command to leave everything you've known behind. But I've heard that in the original language, the phrase has more of a "as you're going along in life" kind of feel. More like Jesus is saying, "As you work and play and live your life, make disciples, which includes telling them the truth about what you have seen and experienced." I love that idea, because I think it matches the way Jesus lived his life. He healed, preached, confronted, and changed the lives of people as he was moving through his life, from one place to another. We see evangelism as something we're supposed to do on a special trip to another country, or some sectioned off part of our life. But it's supposed to be something that we do along the way, as we are going on with our lives. We're at the store, and the checker is open to hearing the truth of Christ in our life. We're talking with a friend who needs the encouragement to trust Jesus. Are those the moments Jesus is talking about here?

WHAT CHALLENGES DO YOU FACE IN TELLING PEOPLE ABOUT JESUS "AS YOU ARE GOING"?

One thing is crystal clear in Jesus' words to the disciples. Evangelism isn't about getting people to declare a decision or repeat a special prayer. It's about encouraging people to trust Christ and committing to join with and help them become disciples. The direction we have from Christ is to go wherever we go in this world, baptizing and teaching people. It's not a call to offer people the four spiritual laws and then let them go face their world on their own. It's a challenge to continue walking with people we love, helping them see the depth of God that we have seen and experienced. Evangelism is not a snapshot of a moment; it's a film that plays throughout our entire lives.

You have to wonder why Jesus doesn't say anything else there, like make sure they get the truths from the Pentateuch. Jesus would have certainly have had the Pentateuch memorized. Why not mention that? Jesus could have said that they needed to cast out demons...why not say that? I don't know why, and I suspect that no one living knows why either. We're to teach the commands of Jesus, not something else. Not our own theology, not our churches doctrine. Nada. Even as I say that, evangelism systems come to mind, ones that have made gospel presentation formulaic and easy to swallow.

The act of evangelizing someone has to be one of the most talked about, published about, and over-programmed things within all of Christendom. There are countless books on the subject, speakers traveling around leading evangelism seminars, and dozens of conferences and workshops, all in hopes of helping Christians do a better job of saving the entire world. But the first and best step forward we can make into effective evangelism is to lose whatever format, structure, plan, steps, laws, or whatever we have been told that "works" in sharing the gospel.

It's time to put away our evangelism kits and unlearn our debating techniques. It's time to stop walking around like big-game hunters who see targets on the backs of everyone who doesn't attend church regularly, use Jesus-speak, or practice the same kind of lifestyle we do.

It's also time to stop thinking evangelism is something we go and do somewhere else, outside of our normal lives. Recently I heard about a local Christian radio station that was giving away a free evangelistic mission trip to an exotic place, just like the ones they give away on non-Christian radio stations. Two lucky winners would get to experience a day of work, a conversation with an unsaved person, and several days of rest and relaxation on the beach. This is what evangelism has become. Is it what Jesus wanted?

I think the answer to our years of flawed evanga-hunting is living a life of love where we live right now. Being Jesus for the people you directly influence. It means standing on your front porch, looking out on your neighborhood and asking, "Who can I love here…and how can I love them?"—and then opening our ears and doing what we think we hear. It means always loving. Always. This is not easy, and in fact, might be the most difficult of all of my little challenges to myself. When I'm driving. When I'm standing in line for movie tickets. When I'm annoyed. It doesn't matter when or where.

WHAT DO YOU THINK MIGHT HAPPEN IN THE LIVES OF YOUR THREE CLOSEST FRIENDS IF YOU COMMITTED TO LIVE A LIFE OF LOVE FOR THE NEXT WEEK?

It's tough to live this way because love gets beyond statistics. This way of love is beyond what we have been taught as the effective mode of sharing Jesus. We've always been told to be loving *as we are telling* his story. But I'm not sure we've ever been told just to love—and to allow our love to be the message.

That's difficult because it levels the playing field. It admits that we need love, and the same kind of love as the love that we are giving out. It admits that we are all needy, that we all need a hug, that we all are dirty.

It's also difficult because there's no detailed program. The method is simple…learn what Jesus did, and then do that. Love people the way Jesus did, without limits. Listen to them. Share honestly with them. And love them.

A LOVE THAT LISTENS

We do so much "talking to" non-believers, wanting them to hear what we have to say, because we believe it is important. It is life changing. And it is. But talking first is not the answer. Love listens before it speaks. What's happening in the life of the person you have befriended? What brings him joy? What makes her heart ache? Until we can drop the format and listen, we've not earned the right to expect to be heard.

Authentic evangelism doesn't tell people how to live, it struggles alongside them. It shares life-journeys together, answering honest questions with honesty. If we expect those we are telling about God to be honest, we have to be honest back. If the person you are speaking with asks if you've ever dealt with lust, responding, "Well, yes, but that's not important," won't work. People ask questions because they want to know if God could really love them. They're not asking so we can expound on our theories of salvation.

WHAT IF EVANGELISM ISN'T ABOUT SPEAKING OR PROCLAIMING AS MUCH AS IT'S ABOUT LISTENING AND LIVING A LIFE OF LOVE? WHAT DIFFERENCE WOULD THAT MAKE?

Not long ago, I took some students from our church on a mission trip to Mexico. The trip was sponsored by a great missions organization that designed an effective week of service for our students. We spent the week helping to rebuild one man's house, walking the streets of the city, and praying for the people who lived in the small houses lining the streets. Part of our job during the entire week was to tell people we met about God.

I loved the idea—but I felt awkward the entire time. We didn't speak the language. We weren't part of that culture. We didn't look like the locals. And yet, we were supposed to tell them we knew what they needed. We were supposed to tell them about Jesus.

I struggled the entire week. The host organization gave us a pretty solid guarantee that our work would be followed up on by the next team or the organization itself. But the guy whose house we helped build and the neighborhood we worked in were so foreign to us—and I'm pretty certain we felt foreign to all the people there.

But maybe when I'm totally honest I have to admit that my struggle with witnessing isn't really about whether North American Christians should be traveling all over the world, sharing the gospel with cultures they don't really understand. Maybe the core of my struggle is that sharing my faith in the traditional evangelistic way always feels too trite. I have to boil down the core of who I am, the substance of what is most important to me, and communicate it in just a few words, so I don't lose my audience before they're able to make a decision. And that, to me, feels like an approach that's focused more on keeping score than on seeking changed lives.

In many ways our week in Mexico was wonderful. It was wonderful because the lives of several students who went on the trip were profoundly changed. It was wonderful because an old man got his house rebuilt for free. It was wonderful because we were able to tell three young Mexican guys about Jesus, we prayed for 27 families in that community, and we lost two soccer games to the locals.

It was a great experience. But I'm pretty sure no one met Jesus because of that trip. And that still kind of bothers me.

CHAPTER

GRACE FOR THE LESS-THAN-GRACEFUL

SIX

For most of my life, salvation was one of the simplest concepts for me. If you knew Jesus, you were saved. If you didn't know him...well, sorry, but you were dead.

And if you pushed me on what it meant to "know Jesus," I'd have given you the prepackaged answer I'd been taught and had heard others say. You pray a prayer, surrender your life to Christ, and the deal is done.

I knew different Christian groups argued about some aspects of this. For example, once a person had prayed that prayer, was he or she saved eternally—or could the deal be broken by sin? This was something

Christians disagreed about. But no one I knew ever questioned the deal itself, the way we got into the Jesus Club.

So I was pretty secure in my thinking about salvation until one day when I heard a famous Christian speaker say, "I've come to the place in my Christian walk where I have to accept that there are nonbelievers who are more Christian than I am." And the more I thought about that statement, the more certain I was that he was right. I'd been looking at salvation from my perspective, from a place where I needed everything tied neatly together. I'd been viewing it from that typically human place where I'd decided how something spiritual happens, and then was pretty sure God thought my way of thinking was correct.

Of course, I'd never really read any passage in the Bible where God says you need to say a particular prayer or that you are saved for forever. But that's what I'd been taught, and my own theology was completely set in place. Salvation was a simple process of realizing your sin and accepting the death of Christ. Either you'd done it or you hadn't. Case closed.

I don't know where I got this idea of a "binary spirituality." But somewhere along the line I came to think of salvation as operating like a computer, where every piece of data and every process, no matter how complex, boils down to a series of ones and zeroes, or yeses and nos. Salvation was as clear and definite as that. Did you say the prayer? Then you were a "one," and you were saved. If not, you were a "zero."

And when I read the Bible's words about *grace*, it was only for the "ones." When I read about *faith*, it was a one also—only for the saved. Same with *forgiveness*. In fact, every positive word I read in Scripture, every promise from God, every assurance of God's love, was only for those who already knew Jesus. God's love and grace came to us after that salvation moment, at the point when the seeker was spared from eternal death and safe in the arms of Jesus. Then he or she was totally and completely changed and permanently unchangeable.

But now I'm convinced that belief is not biblical. There isn't any place in Scripture where Jesus says we have to repeat a certain sentence, and he definitely doesn't tell us what that sentence is. And I cannot fathom that God sees salvation as such a trite, closed-ended thing. The God I know is creative enough to have dreamed up this world, powerful enough to have made it, and loving enough not to let us live brokenhearted. Yet I'd been taught that his decision on whether or not we could spend forever with him rested neatly on a simple one-sentence prayer.

Looking back, I remember confronting this exact issue when I was a new Christian. I think most every family has at least one member they usually don't tell the whole story about. Maybe it's the uncle who's got two DWIs, the cousin who cross-dresses, or the aunt with anger issues. In my family full of pretty conservative Christians, there's one person who is gay. And despite the typical rhetoric I've heard from so many Christians today about how rotten gay people are, and how much God hates gay-ness, I love this person. It's impossible to explain what a conflict this has been for me: Trying to follow Jesus (who I believed would have been a conservative on just about every issue) while still loving my family member who was so clearly non-Jesus-y. I remember praying for him, thinking if he could just experience Jesus the same way I had, he'd turn away from those demonic feelings. I remember feeling so bad for him and his struggles, but so good that I was standing on something so clear and right. And, even though I spent time with this relative and "loved" him, I always felt kind of gross about him. Icky. The fact that he was attracted to someone of the same sex made me feel angry and disgusted all at once.

HOW DO YOU UNDERSTAND SALVATION? WHERE DID YOU GET THAT UNDERSTANDING? HOW DOES YOUR UNDERSTANDING MATCH UP WITH SCRIPTURE?

But I could justify those feelings. And I believed God would use me to save my relative. I imagined my prayer for my relative would change God's mind about him. Even if this relative wasn't spiritually intelligent enough to ever offer that simple "Jesus save me" prayer, God could hear me praying for him—and he'd be saved.

But that binary way of thinking about salvation exploded when I got to college. I went to a Christian college where I assumed no one would be gay. And yet, I met a student who was gay sometime in my first week at school. It was different than with my relative—I loved my family member first and then discovered he was gay. Continuing to love him was somewhat difficult, but made easier by the fact that I knew them. But I didn't have to love this student I'd just met. Of course, I had to be kind, because Jesus would have been kind to him. I had to be willing to hang out with him, because Jesus would have done that, too. Jesus ate with "these kind of people" and, well, I did that too, modeling the behavior of my fearless leader. But I was pretty sure the Bible said somewhere that Jesus didn't *really* love gay people—so I didn't have to love them, either.

But it's not just been these two guys in my life. Several close friends from my college days are gay—and they are also sincerely trying to follow Christ. As a part-time university professor, I often speak with students who feel a longing for relationships with the same sex. For so many years, I would have said these people were lost. In my mind, there was never an in between place where a person was kind of saved, or close to being saved, or journeying toward salvation. There wasn't an island where you can live that's somewhere between not believing in God and "getting there."

But something happened to me that changed all that binary thinking. I started meeting people who were *on their way* to salvation.

It wasn't just these friends who were wrestling with what it meant to be both gay and created in God's image. I discovered musicians who were searching for answers and expressing that search in their music. I caught up with thinkers who seemed to love God and expressed a desire to know more about him, yet had not yet taken that step I felt was so important, that step where they said a prayer accepting Jesus as Savior. I met people in transition toward Christ, but obviously not completely trusting him. I met people who didn't call themselves Christians, yet they lived out Jesus' love and compassion far better than most believers do. I met other people who clearly loved God, and yet some of their lifestyle didn't match how I thought believers should live. I started meeting real people, who lived real lives and struggled deeply with real issues. They didn't spend time worrying about the trivialities that so many church people focus on. Their quest was deeper, and they seemed to look into themselves at a level deeper than I had ever looked into myself.

ARE THERE PEOPLE OR GROUPS THAT YOU THINK OF AS "TOO FAR GONE" TO RECEIVE GOD'S GRACE?

I had to reconcile what I'd been taught about God and salvation with what I knew about these people and their lives. It felt like a difficult math problem where I knew what the answer was, but the answer didn't make sense. If God loves everyone, *really* loves each of us the same way I love my kids, and if he'd do something so daring and dramatic as sending his son to die for them, then why didn't he love them all the way into heaven? I mean, why didn't God love them even if they'd not "said the prayer" we've made up?

Ultimately, all of this boiled down to me reconsidering what I believe. I decided that if I really believed in God's great love for every single one of us (and I do believe that), then I had to open myself to the possibility that God's love was large enough to welcome into his presence people who had not prayed the same way I had. We don't get to decide whom God allows to come to him. Scripture tells us Jesus is the only way. But the Bible doesn't tell us how the acceptance of Jesus happens (or even when it happens).

There isn't a formula for knowing Jesus. While God helps us along with key passages like this one...

> If we claim to be without sin, we deceive ourselves and the truth is not in us. If we confess our sins, he is faithful and just and will forgive us our sins and purify us from all unrighteousness. (1 John 1:8-9)

And this one...

> Then he called the crowd to him along with his disciples and said: "Whoever wants to be my disciple must deny themselves and take up their cross and follow me. For whoever wants to save their life will lose it, but whoever loses their life for me and for the gospel will save it. (Mark 8:34-35)

...but there isn't anything formulaic in Scripture that defines how we get there. And when you read the entire New Testament, you see that people come to salvation in all sorts of ways. The thief on the cross gets there because he tells Jesus he wants to be with him in paradise. The woman at the well discovers him because she's open to Jesus' challenging words. But the people in Scripture don't all follow the same path to Christ. There's no formula. There's just the discovery of a passion for Christ. And that seems to be enough.

DO YOU HAVE BELIEFS ABOUT SALVATION THAT YOU'VE CREATED ON YOUR OWN OR BELIEVE BASED ONLY ON WHAT YOU'VE BEEN TAUGHT? HOW DO THESE IDEAS MATCH UP WITH SCRIPTURE?

We may think we know what someone needs to do to be saved, but, in Paul's words, we only see "through a glass darkly." If judgment is left up to God, then so is acceptance into his kingdom. And although I understand that this may not feel like an "answer" to the salvation question, I have to acknowledge that the whole question of whom God saves (and how he saves them) isn't really up to me.

GRACE THAT'S REALLY AMAZING

I feel like what I've just said is probably a little difficult to grasp. When I reread the words above, part of me wonders if I've dove off into the deep end—or maybe even into the waters of heresy. But I think I'm really diving into something different—a deeper understanding of the concept of grace.

Like every other Christian on the planet, I've spent years talking about the importance of God's grace. I spoke as if I understood what grace was. I taught Bible studies on it. I knew God's grace was free and that Jesus' dying on the cross was the ultimate expression of it. I knew we were blessed as Christians because Jesus paid our price.

But I really didn't *feel* what grace was about until Jacqui and I were expecting the birth of our first child. I couldn't understand the love I felt for this child I'd not yet seen, I just knew I had it. I loved my daughter. I read to her while Jacqui was pregnant, hoping Nicole could hear the sound of my voice through the skin that separated us. I loved her, even though the only image I'd seen of her was from an ultrasound picture. I loved her so completely, so wholeheartedly, that I would do *anything* for that little life inside Jacqui. Our faces had never met, yet I was willing to surrender myself for her.

I felt that same love for her the first moment I saw her face, when she was just minutes old, with big black eyes and wet hair. I felt that same love for her the first time she pooped her diaper and the day she took her first steps. I love her when she ignores my advice and makes mistakes because of it. I love her when she succeeds. There is nothing she could ever do to stop my love for her.

I remember very clearly one of the first times Nicole disobeyed us. She was two, and we were standing near a bus full of high school students, ready to leave for a weekend ski trip in Colorado. Stuff was happening all over the place, and both Jacqui and I had things to take care of, but we needed Nicole to stay where she was safe. I remember Jacqui's words very clearly, asking Nicole not to cross the yellow line that marked the edge of the parking lot. Nicole looked down at the line, then looked back up at Jacqui and me, and stepped over the line into the dangerous parking lot. My love for her did not change as she stood there considering whether she would obey or not. My love for her didn't change the moment she crossed the line. And my love for her didn't change when, after being caught, she wailed at being dragged back behind the line and scolded, refusing both her guilt and our discipline.

Our love for our daughter isn't limited to the times when her behavior pleases us. And I'm certain that's also true of God's love and grace toward us. It's much bigger and more all-inclusive than we tend to assume. Yet I've often tended to think of God's grace as something that gets extended to us only once we've done the right thing. I act as if God's grace toward me began with that moment when I chose to stand up next to God, when I chose to believe in Christ. And I guess I have also believed that, if I ever chose to completely disown Jesus, if I somehow wandered out into the parking lot on my own, God's grace for me would end. I knew God was limitless, but, in my mind, some aspects of his character—specifically his grace—did not feel limitless. People received God's grace only if they seemed interested in God or were about to make that decision to follow him. In my understanding there was no grace for people who obviously didn't care about God.

HOW DO *YOU* DEFINE GRACE?

I am not saying that all Christians think the way I did. But I think an awful lot of us act as if we believe this. Evidence? The things we argue about. Does God love gay people? Does God love the woman who gets an abortion—or the doctor who performs one? Does God love the guy sitting on death row? Does God honor the prayers of a Muslim kid? Does he love the lead singer of a death metal band? We might be quick to say, "Yes, of course, God loves all these people." And yet, we argue over how much, we form committees about whether these people we say God loves are really welcome in our churches, and we struggle to express any kind of openness to those whose beliefs and practices don't match our own.

Although we talk a lot about God's grace, we seem to miss the point of all those stories where Jesus demonstrates it. We love that story about Jesus dining with Zacchaeus (Luke 19:1-10), and the one about him offering living water to the Samaritan woman at the well (John 4:1-26). We think of these passages as motivators for our evangelism (See how good Jesus is? He goes after the worst kinds of people.) when, in reality, he's demonstrating the boundaries of his grace, which actually has no boundaries at all. When we ask God, "How far does your grace go? Whom do you really love?" we have these stories as an answer. It extends to the people *our* grace would never touch, to the people we're willing to toss into hell for living like they do. After all, they're the ones who crossed the yellow line.

But God's grace is much bigger than ours. It makes us uncomfortable. So we let the lines we've drawn around grace and salvation trump how God sees it. In our effort to define who gets saved, we have emptied salvation of all of its meat. We have made it something measurable instead of something beautiful. We talk about salvation as if it were a brass ring to be grabbed while riding a silly plastic carousel horse. And somewhere along the way, our narrow understanding of grace and salvation ruined our witnessing and evangelism. Inviting people to walk with Jesus became a quest to require that they accept our reasoning, philosophy, and holy book on the basis of one 20-minute diatribe. God's grace turned into something that was only for those who were already in the club.

The religious leaders of Jesus' day did the same thing, and it made Jesus furious. They relied on the outward evidence of their salvation, demonstrating their holiness through things like fasting and prayer—

and eventually these religious structures replaced living faith. Before long, following God was not about the journey or the discovery, it was about the rules and definitions. It was about wearing the right clothes, using the right language, and doing the right stuff.

WHEN HAVE YOU DENIED THAT GOD'S GRACE IS FOR THOSE WHO HAVE "CROSSED THE LINE"?

I find it so interesting that Jesus spent so little time with "church people." Instead of hanging out with people who thought they had God all figured out, Jesus actively sought out and passionately loved people the religious leaders never bothered with. And just like those religious leaders, we struggle with what grace and salvation really are. We forget that grace is central to God's character. We forget that God relentlessly pursues and passionately loves even those who don't know about him. We forget that the decision about whom God chooses to love and save is up to God and God alone. We don't get a vote.

I understand the temptation. Defining what salvation is helps us Christians know who's in our club—and who isn't. And it allows us to rail against those we think fall outside the lines. Which brings me back to the way many Christian talk about sexuality—and particularly homosexuality. I hear many Christians say things like, "We're called to love the sinner, but hate the sin." They use big, deep, holy-sounding voices to give these statements more credibility. I hear those words in just about every church conversation regarding the issue. And I've heard a similar kind of thinking and tone about God's attitude toward people of other religions, hungry people, people with cancer or AIDS. We talk about these issues with such certainty, yet we've pieced our opinions together on the basis of random Bible passages and incoherent tradition. And we've completely forgotten that our opinions about these issues don't matter. God is not looking for us to make big decisions for him about what to do with people who don't know him the way we do. He's asking us to model love and extend grace.

GOD'S LOVE AND OURS

When it comes to loving people, I talk a good game. I can spend a lot of time talking about how important it is to love people like Jesus did, but not actually loving like he did. Sometimes I look back and notice that I've been giving lip service to how God calls people (people like *you*) to love everyone. But I've done little loving on my own.

Authentic love reaches out to people whom society has declared unlovable. People like the homeless guy who walks up and down the highway not too far from my house, wearing pants for a hat, and often waving his hands wildly as he talks. Or the unsmiling woman who works the counter at the Burger King near my house and refuses to make eye contact with anyone. Or any of the other people I encounter daily who don't look or act like the kind of people I think Jesus wants in his army.

I've felt held back from loving such for years. I haven't felt held back from *talking about* loving them, but I've definitely not reached out and grabbed that call as my own. That's something I'm working hard to change. I know that the authentic believer loves people as they are. That's what I see in Jesus—a passion for talking with, eating with, and loving the people I avoid. The people I look down on are the people Jesus connected with the most. That guy who stands at the stoplight asking for money. The pregnant woman who has no idea who her child's father is. I think that even if you stripped away Jesus' divinity, you'd still have a guy who demonstrated the way God wants us to treat one another. Did Jesus really need to know someone's heart to know that person was loved by God? I don't think so.

I don't know people's hearts either, and I try to love them. I try. But I often find myself just going through the motions. I find myself trying to love people only because God would love them, but not actually loving them. I say to myself, "Well, God loves that person, I need to try." But I do that without ever really accepting who that person is at all.

That's not love—and it's not authentic. Jesus accepted people for who they were. Authenticity demands that we do the same.

I've struggled to understand how God could love people who don't profess the same faith I do or who don't behave the way I think they should. I don't know why God would choose to make all this such a mystery to me. But I do know that it's the very heart of God to love all of us, even though none of us loves him the way he craves. And I know God loves the guy who used to fix my brakes.

I met him at the gas station. Actually, he forced the meeting. I'd been driving around with squeaky brakes for weeks, maybe even months. I don't know much about cars, not nearly enough to be able to fix them. Our brakes were worn down and making a noise that could wake up the whole neighborhood (and probably did). This guy heard the noise and saw an opportunity.

"Now, you know I ain't needin' to beg anyone for money, but I heard your brakes and you know that ain't no sound your car should be making."

That's the first thing he ever said to me. And, since then, we've had so many amazing interchanges. Our conversations would always start about the brake issues my car has. The price of the pads. The cost for turning the rotors. The labor. But the conversations never ended there. They moved into his life. How many kids he had. Which of his relatives still lived in the neighborhood. What his wife was doing that day. He was missing a few teeth, so every "s" came out a little funny, with his tongue sticking out a bit too much. And every conversation we had was salted with language that would make Jesus cry. But each time we talked I got to know him a little better.

WHAT HOLDS YOU BACK FROM LOVING OTHERS?

I always made small talk and spoke to him like he wasn't very smart because, honestly, that's how I thought of him. He was of the world, and even though he was a huge help to our family, I acted like we were doing him a favor by having him work on our car. Every time I passed his house and saw him, I'd wave—

and I imagined my wave was the highlight of his day. When he'd drive past our house, he'd honk—and I imagined he was just wanting me to know that he's still around, still fixing brakes, and if I needed anything...you know, to call.

Eventually, I learned how to change my own brakes. I didn't need him anymore, and he fell out of my life. I stopped waving and he stopped honking. After a while I didn't see him sitting in front of his house anymore, but I gave it little thought.

WHO IN YOUR LIFE NEEDS TO HEAR ABOUT GOD'S LOVE AND GRACE? WHAT CAN YOU DO RIGHT NOW TO HELP THEM SEE GOD'S LOVE IN YOU?

Then my wife ran into him one day at the corner store where we often shop. He noticed her and struck up a conversation. "Where has your husband been?" he asked. "He didn't come to visit me." And, as they talked more, she understood what he meant.

He told my wife that I'd once said that if there ever came a time when I didn't see him sitting in front of his house anymore, I'd stop by to see what the problem was. Well, it turns out he'd had a heart attack and had been in the hospital for a while. He was pretty sick. He'd expected I'd show up. But I never did.

It's interesting that he didn't ask my wife about our brakes or why we never called on him to fix them anymore. I have no idea why my promise to stop by stuck in his head. I wonder if he thought about it every day while he was laid up, or if it would have made little difference to him. I have no idea.

But I think I let this man's salty language and his

worldliness get in the way of our having a good re-lationship. What if his language didn't matter? What if I hadn't allowed something so silly to prevent a friendship? What if I was supposed to be the way God would show his love for this man, and I completely missed it?

And here's the kicker to all that: Despite the fact that I think this is a really important lesson for me to learn, I still don't know the guy's name.

CHAPTER
HERE'S A SANDWICH (CAN SOMEONE SNAP MY PICTURE?)
SEVEN

In the town where I grew up, we didn't have any homeless people. Homelessness didn't exist then—or, if it did exist, it existed somewhere else. Our town had plenty of bars, and it wasn't unusual to see a drunk sleeping on the park bench in the middle of the day. But by late afternoon they'd disappeared. And there were poor people, of course, but they had homes, too. If there were any homeless people in our small town, their presence was a well-kept secret.

And that's why I never really gave much thought to homelessness. Not really. I guess I knew there were people who lived on the streets, but I never thought about them. And if I had given it any thought, I'd probably have said they were homeless because they were stupid, bad with money, heavy drinkers, or on drugs. Being without a home was their own fault, and they were stupid to let themselves continue to be homeless.

But again, there were no homeless people back when I was younger. Homelessness just didn't exist— at least, not where I grew up.

I didn't really gain any awareness of homelessness until my first year of college when I went to work for the Salvation Army over Christmas break. I traveled to Knoxville, Tennessee, for what would be the first of six Christmas-break jobs with the Salvation Army.

The job was pretty simple, but it was also kind of grueling. You got up every day, dressed yourself warmly, and were carted off to a shopping mall, grocery store, or expensive clothing store. You'd stand outside the store all day, ringing a tiny bell, smiling, and saying "Merry Christmas" and "Thank you!" over and over. Every now and then I even let a "God bless you" slip out, which wasn't really my style. (I've never really been a "God bless you" kind of person.)

I was 19 that first Christmas break, and I assumed the Salvation Army would take good care of me. When I agreed to do the work, I figured they'd have us staying at some hotel in the city. In fact, some of my friends did get bell-ringing jobs in other cities where they were housed in hotels. But we didn't.

I remember arriving in town on a Greyhound bus and being taken immediately to the homeless shelter. "Okay," I thought to myself. "Getting into work immediately. This is good. I'm ready." And I was excited.

I'd been sitting in classrooms for months. A little hard work sounded fun. But my heart sank when our host said, "Grab your bags, and I'll show you where you'll be sleeping." That's how I found out I'd be living in a homeless shelter for the next couple of weeks.

We walked through an office area where we were greeted by both an attractive receptionist and a drooling man with a strange body odor. As the horrifying reality that we were actually going to live there began to sink in, I stepped over a few bodies sleeping in the hall and entered the room I'd be sharing with three of my college buddies.

Over the next several weeks, we were extremely well taken care of by the head Salvation Army officer in Knoxville, and I received a hands-on crash course in homelessness. Yeah, I worked on their behalf, ringing an annoying bell for about 12 hours a day, but as I look back, that's not why I believe God led me to Knoxville. The job could have been done by just about anyone with a brain and a pulse. (Come to think of it, I guess a brain wasn't essential.) But I think God wanted to teach me something, and my teachers were to be the homeless people staying at that Salvation Army shelter.

At some level, I must have recognized this, because I didn't stay cloistered in my room with my buddies most nights. I'd sit out in the lobby, watching the people go in and out, talking with the homeless folks, and listening to their stories. And there were stories. One guy was homeless because his family had rejected him when he told them he was gay. Another man ended up there after his house burned down. There *were* mentally challenged people and folks battling drug or alcohol addictions, but they weren't a significant demographic of the shelter population. These were normal people with normal problems that had been ramped up just a little more than the problems my friends and their parents faced. They were folks who didn't have any safety net to catch them when they stumbled. I imagined that one of them could easily have been an uncle or cousin of mine.

I talked with them, and even more I listened—sometimes late into the night because that's when many of them began showing up. Whenever I needed someone to talk with, all I had to do was open my door because several guys slept in the hallway right outside my room. They were there when I went to bed—and when I woke up the next morning. And, unless I grabbed a burger at a fast food place on my day off, I ate with them.

In those weeks, homelessness took on a personality. It had a face and a story—and that story didn't involve gambling or drugs.

During the next few years, I worked for the Salvation Army in many different cities, and in each place, I received an education they didn't offer me at college. I was working along with people who were living out Jesus' words about feeding the hungry and caring for the poor, doing what I thought was truly God's work.

I rang my small bell at the base of the World Trade Center in New York City, years before the terrorist

DOES THE DISCREPANCY BETWEEN THE RICH AND THE POOR IN THE UNITED STATES MAKE YOU QUESTION THE WAY SOCIETY IS STRUCTURED? HOW DO YOU THINK JESUS MIGHT ADDRESS THE NEEDS OF THE HOMELESS IN AMERICA TODAY?

attacks of September 11. Each day a significant amount of money passed by me in the pockets of rich and influential people heading for Wall Street. But there were plenty of homeless people there, too—lying around the entrance to the towers, in the basement area, by the escalators. It always amazed me that the extremely wealthy and the homeless could occupy almost the same space. Every day I saw rich people walk by homeless people picking through trashcans looking for food.

HOW FAR DO YOU NEED TO TRAVEL TO PUT A FACE ON HUMAN NEED AND INJUSTICE? HOW DOES KNOWING THE PEOPLE WHO ARE SUFFERING CHANGE THE WAY YOU RESPOND?

I got ripped off a few times by homeless people there—including once by a kid trying to "make change" from my bucket (the excuse he used when I caught him). I was asked for money constantly. Poor people yelled at me for refusing to give them the money from the bucket, and rich people yelled at me because I was in their way. My heart was at the same time softened to the struggle of hungry people and annoyed...at how callous people can be, at how rude both wealthy and poor can be. I was aware that not all homeless and hungry people are innocent, and that not every rich person who can afford to give, and give hugely, does.

I know lots of Christians say you should never give money to homeless people because all they'll do is buy drugs or alcohol with it. But as I looked into the eyes of the people asking for money, I didn't see people looking to buy drugs. These people weren't digging through trashcans trying to find cash to buy drugs. They were pulling out discarded gyros and half-finished hot dogs and eating around the bitten parts.

A FAITH WITH LEGS

How we respond to the needs in our world tells the truth about the authenticity of our faith. The truth is told by how we help those struggling through natural disasters. How passionately we seek justice for the poor and hungry around the world. Whether we work to provide safe drinking water, basic vaccines and medical care, and food for all. Those issues define our authenticity. If someone walks up and asks us whether we love Jesus or not, we shouldn't be allowed to just say "yes"—that's too easy. Too often we proclaim our love for God but we never give it legs. When I'm asked whether I love God, I want my answer to be, "Yes—and let me show you what that means. Can you come with me to the community kitchen tonight?"

Again and again in his ministry, Jesus made concern for those in need the litmus test of our faith. He didn't just talk about caring for the poor, he lived among them—and not just on a weeklong mission trip or a day trip to the soup kitchen. Jesus himself was poor, which is one reason he says, "Truly I tell you, whatever you did for one of the least of these brothers and sisters of mine, you did for me" (Matthew 25:40).

There are dozens, maybe even hundreds, of Scriptures that remind us of God's passionate concern for the poor and his expectation that his people will care for the hurts and needs of those around them. Old Testament writers like Amos and Joel take aim at the cold-hearted religious leaders of the time, assuring them that God knows they're ignoring the physical and spiritual brokenness around them. If you need a reminder of God's concern for social justice and his frustration with ineffective religiosity, take a look at these words spoken by God through the prophet Jeremiah:

From the least to the greatest,

all are greedy for gain;

prophets and priests alike,

all practice deceit.

They dress the wound of my people

as though it were not serious.

"Peace, peace," they say,

when there is no peace.

(Jeremiah 6:13-14)

The message echoes throughout the Scriptures from the Hebrew prophets through the words of Jesus and on into our day. God is consistent on the issue of suffering. He hates it, and he expects his people to be about ending it. It's difficult for me to grasp which God hates more—people being hungry or hungry people being ignored by those who say they follow Christ.

We like to think we're doing enough, or that God will ignore or excuse our lack of action. Do we care that he sees what we do and don't do—and knows our hearts? If Jeremiah were alive today, I wonder what God would tell him to write about us?

Some of the Christians I speak with seem to view poor people more as an annoyance than as a reminder of Jesus' words. I hear them say things like, "If he's hungry, he should get a job," or, "I can't even walk to the coffee shop without someone asking for money," or, "Couldn't this guy be sleeping in a shelter somewhere instead of on the sidewalk?" I understand the frustration, yet such words seem so far from the heart of Jesus. These responses to those in need seem so cold and uncaring. How do we get to a place where we no longer care that someone else is hungry?

> WHAT DO YOU THINK JESUS MEANS WHEN HE SAYS THAT WHEN WE SERVE "THE LEAST OF THESE" WE ARE ACTUALLY SERVING HIM?

I'm not saying we should give away everything we have all the time (although that's pretty close to what Jesus tells us). I'm not making a case for emptying our wallets and purses anytime we're asked for money. But I'm saying there are countless people who live among us with no money, no home, and little hope—and it feels heartless to act like they don't exist or their lives don't matter.

We may say we don't want to give money to the guy on the street because we don't want to support a drug habit. But sometimes I wonder if we're saying that to cover up the coldness of our own hearts. How can we know what the man on that street corner will do with the dollar we give him? And if we're concerned he won't spend it the way we'd prefer, well...I imagine the same kind of argument might be made about tithing ("I'm not giving my money to the church. How do I know what they're going to do with it?"), about giving Christmas money to family members ("Did you see their new car? They've got money to burn—they're not getting a Santa card from me!"), and about Christmas bonuses, refunds, or coupons for free food. You can make a logical case for why you should never give anything to anyone. But we don't make these kinds of judgments in most situations. Why do we feel so compelled to scrutinize the spending habits of the homeless?

WHICH IS IT FOR YOU? IF YOU SEE SOMEONE SLEEPING ON THE STREET, DOES IT ANNOY YOU OR BREAK YOUR HEART?

I feel like we often use these kinds of excuses like shields to separate us from the needs that surround us. We pass someone hungry on the streets, and we immediately claim we never give money, we don't help strangers, that handing out money doesn't really help. And, before long we don't even see the homeless guy we walk by every day.

The reality is that giving money does help—at least in that moment. If you feed a person, he's no longer hungry. Feeding someone helps, but it is not the permanent solution for that person.

If we say we care, but we want to be wiser about how we help, then I think it's important to be familiar with the services available in our cities. When someone comes up and asks for food, if I don't want to reach for my wallet, then I need to know where the soup kitchen is where he can get food. I need to be able to direct her to a shelter where she can sleep safely. That's not an attempt to make the homeless someone else's problem. It's an effort to help people find a place where they'll likely get more care than you can provide.

The Bible's message is pretty simple: If we have more than enough, and see others in need, we're expected to give away what we have. Jesus says I can't walk around with two coats and ignore the fact that my brother doesn't have one. The only way to obey God's word is to give things away, and that includes money, food, and clothing. But what freaks me out is that God's call is to do way more that that. And that "more" feels like a call that moves far beyond the way most of us are living right now. God's words in Isaiah here scare me…

Is not this the kind of fasting I have chosen:

to loose the chains of injustice

and untie the cords of the yoke,

to set the oppressed free

and break every yoke?

Is it not to share your food with the hungry

and to provide the poor wanderer with shelter—

when you see the naked, to clothe them,

and not to turn away from your own flesh and blood?

If you do away with the yoke of oppression,

with the pointing finger and malicious talk,

and if you spend yourselves in behalf of the hungry

and satisfy the needs of the oppressed,

then your light will rise in the darkness,

and your night will become like the noonday.

(Isaiah 58:6-7, 9-10)

We don't have to be Bible scholars to know what God is asking of us in Isaiah. And my words would never do justice to the truth that's so clear and easy to find here in Isaiah, and in many other places in Scripture. We are called to share food with the hungry, to provide shelter for the poor, to clothe the naked—but also to do more. See the words there? Loosen the chains of injustice. Untie the cords that bind people. Set the oppressed free. Satisfy needs. For most of us, the real struggle isn't about knowing what God asks of us, the struggle is setting aside our excuses and actually doing the work.

HELPING YOU HELP ME

There's one other related issue here, and it gets back to that pesky question of appearances and our concern about how others view us. It can be extremely easy to use homeless and hungry people to make ourselves look spiritual. Admit it, you're happy to tell the story about the homeless woman you gave a dollar to. And you felt good about sharing the leftovers from your dinner with the hungry guy standing outside the restaurant—and even better about the fact that your friends saw you do it. You love how that looks.

If that's true, you're not alone. We're so good—too good—at using needy people to make ourselves look better. If you want to raise your status in any church, talk about how you're working for the poor, feeding the homeless, or volunteering at the shelter. Jesus said, "The poor you will always have with you" (Mark 14:7). Since then many of his followers have been happy to use this group to our advantage. But Jesus makes it pretty clear that's not what he has in mind...

> So when you give to the needy, do not an-nounce it with trumpets, as the hypocrites do in the synagogues and on the streets, to be honored by others. Truly I tell you, they have received their reward in full. But when you give to the needy, do not let your left hand know what your right hand is doing, so that your giving may be in se-cret. Then your Father, who sees what is done in secret, will reward you. (Matthew 6:2-4)

I think Jesus knew people like us would one day walk the earth. People who will do the right thing and help someone out, but then later in the day make sure to work what they've done into a conversation they're having with someone. That dollar we give to the homeless guy is like an investment that we can draw on later. The hungry per-son becomes collateral, used to one-up our friends' spirituality. I hear people doing it all the time—in fact, I do it all the time.

WHAT CAN YOU DO TO ADDRESS THE SOCIAL NEEDS IN YOUR OWN COMMUNITY?

But when we use our giving to needy people as an opportunity to brag about our efforts, we dehuman-ize them and reduce who they are and what they are struggling through. I don't want to do that. Instead, I want to give the way Jesus commands that we give, in secret, so no one knows what we're giving or when we're giving it.

COMPASSION FATIGUE

Near where I live, there's long been a certain guy who's always standing at the same five-light inter-section. Steve would be there, rain or shine, right at the white line where you stop to wait for the light to change. After we gave him money several times, he began sharing his story with us each time we'd stop. He'd lost his job. He didn't have a home. He was hungry. And we did our part helping him. The questions ran though my head: Was the guy an ad-dict? Why didn't he find another job? Wasn't there a limit to how much I should give a stranger? But each time I saw Steve standing there, Jesus' words about meeting him in the homeless and the hungry ran through my head, and I couldn't ignore them. I felt called to give to him.

Then they put in a Wal-Mart about a hundred yards from the intersection. And with the increased traffic from the new business, other homeless peo-ple started showing up there. Now, at almost every one of the five lights near our new Wal-Mart, there's someone sitting or standing with a sign asking for money or a needy look. Sometimes they walk up and down the row of cars along the median, giving us a close look at their hunger. Sometimes they just stand there looking a little out of it and a lot dirty.

Now I've been a bleeding-heart kind of person for a lot of my life. It's not been that uncommon for me to buy lunch for someone I don't know and drop it off wherever they were standing. I've often been the guy who reaches for his wallet when a needy person asks for money. It's important for me to say that because I've known a lot of people who feel repulsed when asked for money by a stranger. That's not me, or it hasn't usually been me.

But recently, I've noticed a change in my own reaction. I used to welcome seeing Steve at that corner, but these newer people at the intersection are a real eyesore. I can't stand the sight of them. They make me frustrated. Did Steve tell his friends that the people at these lights were an easy mark, and now every homeless person in our city is showing up for handouts? Are they really hungry? Or does our intersection provide easy money and quick access to the alcohol stores close by? Jesus' words about his presence in the needs around us have not changed, but my attitude has. I don't like these people any more. I don't trust them. I think they are lying.

HOW DO JESUS' WORDS IN MATTHEW 6:2-4 IMPACT YOUR SERVICE TO THOSE WHO ARE POOR OR IN NEED?

I have to admit that I've felt almost saintly writing about the problem of homelessness in the world. It feels good to get this chapter out of me. I suspect every person who reads it will feel a little convicted because all of us could do more than we do. It felt good to write about how I'd sit up at night and talk to the guys staying at the shelter. It made me sound almost like Mother Teresa, didn't it? You might even get the idea that I went back to college and became a champion of the cause of ending homelessness. Or that I've made it my life's pursuit since then to help homeless people, giving countless hours in soup kitchens and shelters or continuing to work with the Salvation Army in their fundraising efforts.

But the reality is that my heart has hardened to the plight of homeless and hungry people. I know Jesus commanded us to reach out to those in need of help, but seeing so many with their hands out, and knowing my own struggles to feed my own family, I've stopped caring. I've stopped using the information I received from my experiences. I used to be deeply troubled by the sight of a man digging someone else's half-eaten bagel out of the trash. I've had enough experience to know that homeless and hungry people aren't all thieves or drunks. But I'm not moved anymore. I think that breaks my heart the most.

IS SERVING THE POOR OPTIONAL FOR FOLLOWERS OF CHRIST?

CHAPTER
WHEN IT'S ALL GOD'S FAULT
EIGHT

The church I attend supports dozens of missionaries in countries all over the world. Unlike some congregations whose missionary connections are little more than a few black and white pictures tacked to a "Notes from the Field" bulletin board, we have built strong relationships with the missionaries we support. We're always one of the stops on their schedules when they return to the States. The missionaries we hear from each year bring amazing stories of God's work in the countries and cultures where they minister.

Before I worked at this church, I had a very different understanding of what missionaries do. I figured they preached a lot, read the Bible outside with nearly naked natives, and ate weird food. I've learned a lot in the last ten years. The missionaries I've come to know are spiritual entrepreneurs, seeking to find all kind of ways into the hearts and souls and minds of the people they're serving.

Some of these missionaries are spiritual heroes to me. One family has worked tirelessly for more than 20 years translating the New Testament into the language of the local people. Another couple chose to spend the first few years of their married life as Bible teachers in service to God overseas rather than building their academic resumes here at home. And still another couple have spent their entire adult lives working in airplane hangers and schoolhouses overseas, serving missionary pilots. I've heard the stories of so many other fine missionaries that I feel I'm cheating my friends by mentioning only these three families.

Two good friends of mine recently heard God's call and took up the challenge to move to another country and work with students there. To be honest, I was not thrilled. I understand the importance of God's call, and I honor it. But these were good friends. Kevin and Ruth had both taught each of my kids for a few years, and in that time they'd become personal encouragers to our family. These were true friends, and we shared many good times together. When I learned that they felt called to another country, to do there exactly what they had been doing here in our school, I was disheartened. They were already serving God; did they really need to drop everything and go to another country to do that? What could they accomplish there that they could not accomplish here? I felt confused—happy that they felt a strong sense of

God's call yet sad that these good friends would soon be leaving.

The days of preparation and fundraising and packing went too quickly. They moved late in the summer, at a time when I was attending camp with some students. I grieved through that entire camp, wishing I could have been there to wave good-bye and tell them how much I loved them.

We were worried for them because we knew Ruth needed surgery. She decided to have the surgery done in the country where they were going to work, just before their first year at the new school began. We did what most Christians do when a friend is having surgery. We were concerned, maybe even worried, yet felt confident of God's care. We prayed that the surgery would go well. I guess that didn't work, because we got a call two days after her surgery informing us that Ruth died in recovery.

Now I know that when someone dies, it's important to reach out to that person's family. I wanted to offer support to Kevin. But I could not shake the impact not seeing Ruth again was having on my family and me. I know this may sound selfish, but I was just overwhelmed that we would never get to see her infectious smile again or hear what she'd been reading in her Bible.

I wasn't the only one missing her. There were about 700 people at her funeral. But I wondered if I was the only one blaming God for her death, angry that he'd allowed it, and feeling like he'd just made one of the biggest mistakes of his career.

It's been months, and I still think often of Ruth and the family she left behind. And I've decided that there are some life stories that just don't make sense, and we have a right to blame God for them.

GOD'S CHARACTER

WHAT HAS BEEN YOUR RESPONSE TO TRAGEDY? HOW DID YOU DEAL WITH IT? WHERE DID YOU SEE GOD IN THAT SITUATION?

What happened to Ruth didn't fit with my theology, the neatly created throne I'd constructed for God. A God who would allow Ruth's death—or maybe even *cause* Ruth's death—just didn't match up with who I knew God to be. I had a clear idea of who God was. In my mind, God was like a perfect sunset, one that could never be duplicated. He was more than any human definitions could contain, and yet I'd adopted many of the words we humans have used to define God. Words like...

OMNIPOTENT. This means God is all-powerful. I've always believed God could do anything he chooses to do—and that his power was always consistent with his character. In my college philosophy class, we used to ask our prolifically published, highly intelligent professor if God could create a rock he could never lift. And our prof would wisely respond, "No, because God is *logical* power." I've long believed God would do nothing irrational with his power. We see that in the Old Testament, where God used his power to help Israel at certain times (yet not at other times), and also in the New Testament, where Jesus makes choices about how he will and won't use his power.

OMNISCIENT. God knows everything. A lot of times, when I hear Christians describe this characteristic, it sounds like they're talking more about Santa than God, more of a "He sees you when you're sleeping, he knows when you're awake..." kind of thinking. For me, it means God knows what has happened in the past, he knows what is happening now, and he knows the future.

OMNIPRESENT. God is everywhere all the time. This means God is on our planet and also on Mars and also on the planets in other galaxies. He's here with me as I type, and with you as you read, and in the hospital with my friend who's just had surgery, and with my other friend who's in China right now. I don't, by the way, have any problems with statements like "God is in everything" or "God is in the entire universe." I know some people don't like such words because they think it sounds like a New Age understanding of God, but really, I don't care. It's not within me to try to define what the words "God is everywhere" don't mean.

PERSONAL. God wants to interact with us. We know his name, and he knows ours—which is an intimate way of knowing someone. Perhaps God knows each of us by the names our parents gave us, or maybe God addresses us with another name that represents who we truly are, a name we'll discover one day when we are with him. God as a personal being is incredibly important to me, and I believe Scripture is filled with stories expressing God's personal nature. God reveals who he is in his Word and in our lives because he wants us to know him.

LOVE. God is love—it's one of the foundations of our faith. God acts always for our good. He does nothing for himself and instead always acts on our behalf. I believe he created us because he wanted to love us. The New Testament uses the word *agape* to describe God's selfless love for us, and I think it's a love that was demonstrated in the acts of Jesus and his willingness to go to the cross. But that love didn't begin on the cross, and it doesn't end the moment we choose to surrender ourselves to him. God's love is an enduring love, sticking with us even when we make choices not to continue with him. It's a blanket love, loving us before our surrender and after our death. It's an accepting love, and it doesn't see incorrect beliefs or imperfect lifestyles as a hindrance to being loved.

DO YOU SEE ANY CONFLICTS BETWEEN WHAT YOU BELIEVE TO BE TRUE ABOUT GOD AND THE REAL WORLD THAT SURROUNDS US? IF SO, WHERE?

I wanted to offer you these five words that describe God, because I believe there is truth in them. But I also want to say this. These words—and anything else we might write or say about God—are attempts to describe and understand God, who cannot be fully described or understood. We know this, yet we often end up putting too much faith in our own attempts to describe God. The words we put forth to try to understand God become barriers. In an effort to understand God, we end up describing him to death—and run the risk of ending up with an image of what we want God to be, instead of what God truly is.

I've also found that these definitions of God, which work so great in my head, don't truly work themselves out so well in the real world. They may tell us some small portion of who God is, but they do not tell the whole story of God. And these definitions really don't work for me when I meet someone who...

...is physically disabled

...is clinically depressed

...is extremely lonely

...is plagued by a chronic disease like cancer or a failing kidney

...is mired in debilitating poverty

...is living a life ruined by sin

...is suffering unspeakable emotional or physical pain

The pain and suffering in this world sometimes challenges everything we say we believe about God. Life doesn't always make sense—and it can shake our faith. It can leave us questioning what we think we know about God. Are those definitions lies? Mistakes? Half-truths? How does our understanding of God connect with the world in which we live? If God really is everything I've described, where is he in tragedy? And I mean, *Where is he really?*—not, *Where can we assume he is?* or, *Where have we been taught he is?*

I live through moments where, after hearing stories about starving people in war-torn countries, about people who are dying for lack of clean drinking water, about the hopelessness and despair some people experience with their employment, and on and on, I stop believing God is love, and I start wondering if maybe God isn't just plain disinterested in what's happening in our lives. If God cares, why does he stand back and watch us suffer? If God is all-powerful, why doesn't he intervene? And how can I worship and love this God who seems willing to watch idly as lives fall apart?

I'm not asking, "Why do bad things happen to good people?" That question makes no sense to me. Evil happens to all of us for a lot of reasons—because we've been stupid, because others make terrible choices, because evil is alive and well.

IS GOD'S PERMITTING TRAGEDY OUR CLUE TO STEP IN AND TAKE ACTION?

My question is: What do we do about it? How do we respond? And how do we know that God cares about the evil that surrounds us? And if God does care, why does he only seem to care some of the time?

I guess ultimately I'm asking: If God is love, why isn't my friend Ruth still alive?

EXPLAINING TRAGEDY

We have a lot of different explanations we use when tragedy strikes. We may claim it was due to our sin. We decide that God is using this experience to teach us something. We remind ourselves that God gave people free will, and that our actions have consequences that can affect not just us but others. We talk about the fact that evil is rampant. But we never talk about how those explanations all are completely counter to God's loving, omnipotent nature. We believe, at the same time, in a God who is all-powerful and all-loving, but who also lets us live with extreme tragedy and pain. And, for me, I struggle with loving a God who is so powerful and intimately in our lives, and yet allows us to suffer great hurt—or even causes that hurt. Why would God birth us into such pain? I don't understand how love and those realities fit together. It does not make any sense to me. If I told my kids I loved them, and then allowed them to walk onto a busy interstate, I'd be considered psychotic. So why isn't God thought of as psychotic?

Two stories from Scripture come to mind as I think about this. The first is from John 5, where Jesus finds a man lying near a pool that was known to have healing power. The people believed the first person to make it into the water after it was stirred would be healed. The man has been lying there for 38 years, waiting for his chance—but his chance never comes. Jesus finds him and tells him to pick up his mat and walk. Later Jesus encounters the same man in the temple and says, "See, you are well again. Stop sinning or something worse may happen to you" (John 5:14).

The second biblical story that strikes me as relevant is the moment where Jesus and his disciples see a blind man and the disciples ask Jesus, "Rabbi, who sinned, this man or his parents, that he was born blind?" (John 9:2). Before healing the man, Jesus responds:

> "Neither this man nor his parents sinned," said Jesus, "but this happened so that the works of God might be displayed in him. As long as it is day, we must do the

works of him who sent me. Night is coming, when no one can work. While I am
in the world, I am the light of the world."
(John 9:3-5)

I think that first story represents the way I think
most of us think about the bad stories that we encounter. We think the serious issues people struggle
with are connected to sin. We see the homeless guy
living on the streets and wonder what awful thing he's
done to find himself in such a desperate situation. I do that—don't you? I assume it's his
fault. I assume it's the result of sin—and if
he doesn't quit sinning, it'll only get worse.

**DOES KNOWING
THAT SUFFERING CAN
REVEAL GOD'S GLORY
HELP WHEN YOU SEE
SOMEONE SUFFERING?**

We see that same view reflected in the
disciples' question in that second story: "Who
sinned that this man was born blind?" But I
think Jesus' response to that question offers
a glimpse of the way God looks at the broken
person or the bad story. It's for his glory.

If that sounds conciliatory to you...well,
you're right. I do believe God reveals his
glory and demonstrates his mercy in the midst of our
brokenness and struggles. But, honestly, I don't fully
believe that's why the suffering exists. I believe Jesus
is speaking the truth here, but that truth doesn't always work itself out in the real world. There are dozens and dozens of stories that start bad, end bad, and
are filled with badness. There are too many stories of
brokenness that don't end in God's miracle-working
power being exposed to the world. What are we to
make of those stories where God doesn't step in and
fix things? Are there just too many problems? Is he

incapable of fixing them all? Is he uninterested? Does our sin or our denial of his power in our lives prevent him from acting—as if God needs us to admit his power before he could use it? What happens when things aren't worked out, when there isn't a lesson to be learned from the tragedy, when the man born with no arms isn't able to paint with only his toes, when the teacher dies before her missionary life really starts? I don't want to know where God is when bad things happen. I want to know why he isn't consistently working out the stories of the broken people.

I've always thought of God as the Ultimate Mr. Fix-It. God steps in and takes the broken stuff of our lives and makes us whole again. I imagine that's a pretty common understanding among many Christians in America. Yet I'm not sure that's really God's character. Does he always want to fix things and make us whole? What if, in God's omnipotence, he wants some of us to have rotten stories? Does God needs some of us to stay broken, so he can use our misery to show off his glory? If so, is that loving?

I've often heard people say, "God will never give you more than you can handle." Honestly, that might be one of the most frustrating Christianized-catch-phrases I've ever heard. After observing people for years, listening to their stories, and sharing in their struggles, I've learned that phrase is an untruth—and it leads to all kinds of guilt. If we encounter something that is so big that it sinks us into depression, hopelessness, and bad decisions, did God make a mistake and give us more than we could handle? Or is the only explanation that we've failed? Nearly all struggling Christians

I know assume the problem is their lack of faith, their failure, because they've been told God always gives us the resources to handle whatever he's dealt us. I just don't believe it. I think all kinds of stuff happens to us in this world—sometimes for God's greater purposes but sometimes for no reason at all. Every struggle we face might be a great learning or testing opportunity, but it's not always from God. The dark clouds that storm into our lives don't always have silver linings. The simple truth is that we don't always know what God is up to. We don't always know why he allows what he does.

I understand that the "holy" thing to do would be to admit that we don't always understand God's ways and leave it at that. But, to be honest, that's not enough for me. I want to be able to express my anger about the stories that don't work themselves out. I want to rage at God for the kids who die too soon. I want to cry out, "Why?" I want to feel the freedom to tell God that I think he's wrong, to say that I think he missed an opportunity to reach in and make someone whole, to offer life and hope in the midst of so much death and despair.

I don't think it's wrong to want to say these things to God. In fact, I think we need to say these things when we are feeling them. We're reluctant to let loose because we feel that our anger at God isn't holy or respectful—but I honestly believe it can be both.

And it can also be a way we can learn and grow. If all we do is tell God how much we don't like his decision, if all we do is shout, we've just created a one-sided anger diatribe. But if we say what we have to say and then stop and listen to what God might be saying back to us, that feels healthier. We need to be open to yelling our hearts out at God, but we need to be open to hearing back from God in response. And listening means paying attention to silence and noise and images and sermons and music and poetry and anything else God might use to speak to us.

BLESSING AND CURSES

When you read and study the Old Testament, you discover something theologians call Deuteronomic theology, which isn't as difficult to understand as it sounds. In fact, it's pretty simple: When Israel obeyed God, she was blessed, and God rewarded her with victory in a war or some other physical blessing. However, if Israel disobeyed God, misfortune would come upon the people. When things were going well, it was because the people had obeyed God. And when things went badly, it was because they'd failed to do so. There are lots of Scriptures that seem to support this understanding of how the world works.

HOW COMFORTABLE ARE YOU IN TELLING GOD YOUR HONEST FEELINGS ABOUT THE SUFFERING IN OUR WORLD AND IN YOUR LIFE? WHAT WOULD YOU SAY TO HIM RIGHT NOW?

It's clear that Jesus didn't buy the idea that every good situation was proof of God's blessing and every problem was the result of sin. Yet many Christians still believe that if you're blessed financially, then it's because you've been obedient, and God *loves* you. And if someone is physically sick, emotionally troubled, or economically disadvantaged, either we have no explanation, or we say it's the result of sin. The person bound to the chair, the ward, or the bottle might be to blame, but God stands there wearing bulletproof body armor.

Yet such an oversimplified theology doesn't really make total sense in real life. Each day I see the omniscience and omnipotence of God crash against the unanswered suffering that surrounds us. God seems too often silent in suffering, choosing not to put his powerful hand in the mix of the problem, refusing to put the pieces back together. I live with my anger at God's apparent refusal to intervene on behalf of the people he so loves.

I know suffering is much bigger than the death of my friend Ruth. I know people suffer all over the world. Teenagers are killed by drunk drivers. Children starve to death. People are oppressed by evil governments. They're born without limbs. They struggle with addictions, with sexuality, with abuse. Just about every evil I can think of has been carried out by Mother Nature, God, Satan, or evil humans.

But when I really push myself, when I consider the way I've lived my entire life, I have to say that I've often lived like the suffering of other people didn't matter. Of course, I say that it matters; I even believe it matters. But I haven't done anything about it. I've talked about people who are hurting in places like Africa, but I haven't gone there to see if I can make a difference, I haven't given money, and I've often flipped the channel when the story comes on the news. I've removed myself from the problem, offering just enough lip service to make me seem compassionate. But by saying that I care, yet doing nothing about it, I've denied that people really suffer.

I want to live differently. I want to address the suffering I see. Does that mean I'll spend every day getting cups of cold water, sitting beside a casket, and listening to tears? Could it be that there really is a gift in our being able to see suffering? Is it possible that God allows suffering in our world precisely so his people can respond to it? Is God asking us to be his hands, ministering to the pain and hurt and suffering in our world? Is that what it really means for the church to be the Body of Christ?

WHAT COULD YOU DO TODAY TO HELP RELIEVE THE SUFFERING YOU SEE?

CHAPTER
WHEN GOD IS SILENT
NINE

Among the most difficult experiences of my life as a believer are those times when, despite all my efforts to connect with him, God doesn't return the favor. He is silent. He chooses not to talk. At all. For long lengths of time.

I've learned that if I want to have any sanity in my life, I need to expect that God will not, does not, talk back to me. If I expect that God will talk, and he doesn't, then I'll go completely nuts. The reality, at least for me, is that sometimes God chooses not to say anything at all. I know that might not feel very revolutionary. But realizing it was, for me, like discovering an ancient Egyptian artifact.

It might sound silly to say we want to hear God speaking to us—kind of like a psychotic person who claims to hear voices. But I think part of understanding God as our loving heavenly Father is that we expect he will always talk to us, or want to talk to us. And when that's our expectation, and we do not hear from him, it must mean we have a big problem.

But I have to say there have been more times when I haven't heard God than when I have. I'd pray and seek some kind of response from God—and get nada back. In those moments God felt so cold and uncaring. It was like my prayers were just bouncing off the ceiling and the walls and bouncing off of our bodies, too.

I remember one such time, when I was at the end of long emotional journey. Two years earlier, I'd taken a new job and moved my family a thousand miles away from our comfortable life in East Texas to what now felt like the barren deserts of New Mexico. But after living and working there for two years, I hated everything...my job, my house, my car. I hated that we were too poor to buy diapers for our kids. Everyone I hung out with noticed that I hated everything, and they started hating me back for my bad attitude.

I cloaked my life with a ton of hate, so I wouldn't have to face the fact that I'd spent much of my life in a cave searching for the candle of God's will. When we moved to New Mexico, it was because I thought I'd found that candle, after looking for it for so long. I thought I'd finally found that hidden treasure, in the form of a good job working with good people. But, after a few years, I realized I hadn't found anything like a treasure. I felt angry, and frustrated, and I hated pretty much everything.

I did what I thought a Christian should do in my situation. I tried to "discover God's will." I prayed. I think I prayed more in that difficult place than at any other moment in my life. I fasted. I sought advice. I used that old Christian metaphor and looked for open doors. I laid facedown in the sanctuary at my church. I read the stories of Old Testament characters like Moses and Joshua, whose lives were interrupted and altered by God, and tried my hardest to make them apply to my life. I did everything I could think of to seek God's guidance.

HAVE YOU EVER CALLED OUT TO GOD AND HEARD NOTHING BACK? WHAT DID YOU DO?

But I heard nothing. Not a shout, not a voice, not even a whisper. No vision of God's face, no wise sage with an undeniably divine message. No open door or clearly marked path. No answers to why I felt so out of place, so outside of God's will, when I had so diligently sought him.

All I wanted from God was some direction. Should I move my family? Should we stay? I didn't need to know the whole plan—just the next step. I didn't think that was too much to ask.

In the midst of my desperation and God's silence, I decided the best, most spiritual thing I could do was to devote myself more deeply to God. I would *listen* more carefully, *try* harder, and *seek* him more urgently. If I wasn't hearing God, clearly the problem was that I was wrong or sinful. And as I listened and sought, I decided I needed to go off into the desert by myself so I could really hear God's voice.

I don't know why I decided to do that. I guess going into the desert to listen for God just seemed kind of...biblical. I'd never met anyone who'd ever heard God's voice in the desert. But I had this image of myself sitting in the sand surrounded by weeds and rocks and praying aloud to God—and eventually hearing his voice.

So one day I grabbed a bottle of water, drove to the most isolated area I knew of, hiked into the desert, sat down, and started praying. I stayed there for what felt like forever, but really it was just about two or three hours. A few hikers walked by, but for the most part I was alone. Waiting.

I built an altar out of the rocks lying around me. I piled the rocks up and I said to God these words, "You have been silent too long. I feel worthless and used up, and I feel like all my crying out to you has made you giggle more than it has persuaded you to react to my pain. If I can't hear you speak, then why should I even live?"

I wish there was something that came after that. I wish I could say that, as a result of my devotion, God did something. That he spoke to me in the desert so very clearly that I knew exactly what to do. Or that a white horse galloped up and spoke to me in a language only I understood. Or a bush caught fire. Even though I'd committed to stay there until I heard him speak, he never spoke. I never really heard his voice. I looked around a lot. I prayed some more. But I never heard God's voice.

Eventually, our family decided to move and began a new life in the town where my wife had grown up. Because God gave me no clear answer, I went after the most logical one I could scare up. Lacking any direction from God, I made my own decision.

I understand that God doesn't owe us anything. But it sure would help if, when we face life's bigger decisions, we could be sure he'll meet us halfway. I struggle with loving a God who speaks only when he's ready and not when I need him to. I ache through those long silences from God when he seems to care little about my future. I struggle with even wanting to be associated with a God who allows other voices and messages to speak louder than his does.

IF YOU'VE EVER LISTENED FOR AN ANSWER FROM GOD AND HEARD NOTHING, HOW DID YOU UNDERSTAND THAT EXPERIENCE? DID YOU ASSUME THERE WAS A PROBLEM WITH YOU? A PROBLEM WITH GOD?

My experience of God's silence is something I almost never talk about. I rarely speak about it, because I don't want to endure a litany of explanations about where God is, why he's silent, or what sin I might have committed to cause his silence. Honestly, if you tell people that God is talking to you, you look like a spiritual giant. Tell them you've waited and prayed and listened, and never heard anything from God, and you're judged.

LIVING THROUGH THE SILENCE

Twelve years after that moment in the desert, I still have no idea where God was at that time when I needed him. I want to tell you that I now understand exactly what God was doing in my life through that entire experience—and in those other times when I've needed to hear him and he felt silent. I want to say that I now know that God was speaking loud and clear, guiding me, and I just wasn't seeing it. That's what I *want* to say—but I can't. And, honestly, it feels so good to admit that. It feels right to acknowledge that God is not always neat and tidy, that he does not always step in like the hero of the story.

As I look back, I can understand that God was probably working hard, but not in ways I could see. Was he working in my thinking, emotions, and finances? Was he working through the people who offered me wise advice—as well as the ones who were driving me up the wall? Was he working in the real estate agent who took on the task of selling our mobile home as his personal mission, in the church that would eventually hire me, in the people who owned the house we would rent and eventually buy, in the university where I would eventually teach, and in the publishing companies that would eventually see my book ideas and publish them? I can see now how God may have been active in all those areas—nudging and cajoling and twisting and smoothing things out—even as I called on him and heard nothing in response.

I look back on that entire experience and this Scripture comes to mind...

> In the same way, the Spirit helps us in our weakness. We do not know what we ought to pray for, but the Spirit himself intercedes for us with groans that words cannot express. And he who searches our hearts knows the mind of the Spirit, because the

Spirit intercedes for the saints in accordance with God's will. And we know that in all things God works for the good of those who love him, who have been called according to his purpose. (Romans 8:26-28, NIV)

I know some of us have heard that Scripture so many times that it's hard to hear anything fresh in those words. But it's meaningful to me as I look back on those times of God's silence. It reminds me that—as I was praying through my pain, and trying to pray, and even when I felt I couldn't pray—the Holy Spirit was watching what I was living through, telling God about it, and God was acting. God wasn't acting like I expected him to act, like I'd been taught he would act, like I felt I needed him to act. But God was working out everything that needed to be worked out, so that his good in my life could be accomplished.

THINK ABOUT THE THING YOU STRUGGLE WITH THE MOST. HAVE YOU SENSED THE HOLY SPIRIT INTERCEDING ON YOUR BEHALF?

I look back and see that I expected God to be a bit more like Yoda. I expected he'd show up whenever I needed him, do his best to train and teach me in his ways, and make sure I was prepared to tackle whatever challenges he led me to. This Yoda-God was my sage, my mentor, and if I ever got in over my head, he was also pretty darn good with a lightsaber. But this Yoda-God always came at my biding.

I've learned that when we expect this from God we limit our ability to actually follow him. If God is just a wise sage, we can ignore him and opt for another sage who will tell us more of what we want to hear or teach us what we feel we need. We reduce God to something less than the life-giving, brain-molding, future-shaping Creator of all that is.

In my struggle with not hearing God, and in my fighting to make meaning out of not hearing him, I'm beginning to understand that God isn't just the guy who stands on the deck of the ship tossing life vests to drowning people. The scenario isn't, "I am hurting, I rub bottle, God pours out like a genie and grants my wishes." God didn't gather into himself the wisdom of the universe just so he'd be ready to offer me some advice to make it through my next life lesson. God isn't sitting around like an on-call nurse waiting for us to ring when we think we need something.

We get God's nature all mixed up. He is not bound by time or space or need. He's not forever running from this task to that disaster. I am learning that God is our ever-present Reality. He does not float in when we need him, because he never left. He does not offer wisdom now and then, because he is Wisdom. He does not just work for our good; he is all things worked out for good.

This isn't me grasping at straws so I can feel better about God's silence. This is me beginning to grasp a bit more of the true nature of God's character. This is me realizing that God's constant work for our good does not always equal measurable results in the immediate. It doesn't always mean our pain will go away, that our situations will be resolved, that we'll see an immediate change or hear an answer. God is actively working for our good. And that is true in those moments when we can see and understand some of what God is doing—and when God is working in ways that only God knows.

I sincerely believe that. But that doesn't mean I won't complain when God feels silent and far away. I understand that my life truly is not my own, that I am God's. And yet, God has given each of us a life, and he's told us to live that life with passion. When things are not right, when we need a rescue and do not receive it, it's important that we say to God that we are not happy.

IS IT WRONG TO COMPLAIN TO GOD? DO WE NEED TO COMPLAIN TO GET GOD'S ATTENTION?

God never says we are supposed to handle him with kid gloves and never say how we really feel. I understand God's holiness, but does that holiness mean we should never say that we feel forgotten or ignored or frustrated?

I don't know why we think we should be afraid to express our hearts to God. Clearly, the writers of Scripture didn't feel that way. Take a look at the Psalms. None of the psalm writers—David or anyone else—hold back their feelings. You never get the idea that these writers are speaking gently and carefully to God. When the world feels full of God's glory, they sing with joy. But, when it doesn't, they don't hold back...

My God, my God, why have you forsaken me?

Why are you so far from saving me, so far from the words of my groaning?

My God, I cry out by day, but you do not answer, by night, but I find no rest.

(Psalm 22:1-2)

I probably don't need to tell you that this isn't the last time these first few words appear in the Scriptures. Jesus prays this very same Psalm to express his anguish from the cross. In that moment when he felt farthest from his heavenly Father, Jesus clearly didn't think he needed to protect God from his despair. If there are moments when we feel abandoned, we can be sure God can handle our feelings.

EMBRACING DOUBT

When God's silence is loud, I doubt. I know a lot of believers turn to contemplative prayer to seek God's face. I know others turn to their pastors for reflection. Not me. When I do not hear God, and after I've waited and waited for him, my mind easily wanders into that deserted place we Christians often fear. I question his existence. I'm skeptical of his love. I let loose of the hand I thought I was holding, and I easily entertain thoughts that I end up feeling guilty about: *What if I stopped following him—he doesn't care anyway. What if the reason I'm not hearing from God is because he stopped caring for me a long time ago?*

WHAT DOES IT MEAN THAT JESUS PRAYED THIS PRAYER? IS IT POSSIBLE THAT GOD NEVER INTENDED OUR CONVERSATIONS WITH HIM TO BE GUARDED OR SANITIZED?

I feel uneasy telling you that, because some believers consider doubt to be the worst of all sins. Personally, I don't think that's true. I'm not sure doubt is a sin at all. I believe doubt often marks the growing points of our faith. Sometimes I think doubt is more the texture of my walk with God than certainty is. I'm convinced most of us doubt, but I know that very few of us are honest about it.

I also think doubt is a much more prevalent theme in Scripture than we tend to admit. I think nearly all of us are a mixture of faith and doubt. We're like the father of the boy whom Jesus heals in Mark's gospel. When Jesus tells the man that all things are possible for those who believe, the man responds, "I do believe. Help me overcome my unbelief" (Mark 9:24). We believe—and yet we struggle with doubts and questions.

I love the story of how John the Baptist, after he was imprisoned, began to wonder if he'd been completely wrong about Jesus. We're talking about a guy who went around telling the world that a savior was coming and then had the privilege of being the one to baptize Jesus in the Jordan River. And yet, in the darkness of a prison cell, his certainty begins to fade. Matthew's gospel tells us, "When John heard in prison what the Messiah was doing, he sent his disciples to ask him, 'Are you the one who was to come, or should we expect someone else?'" (Matthew 11:2-3).

I wonder if really understand the impact of John's experience with doubt. John was the one who should have fully grasped Jesus' identity. He was Jesus' cousin. He had clearly been called to tell the world Jesus was coming. He had a front row seat when the Spirit came down on Jesus and God's voice declared, "This is my Son, whom I love" (Matthew 3:17). John certainly understood from his own experience who Jesus was—or at least he should have understood. He'd given his whole life to preparing the way for Jesus.

But, in prison, John begins to doubt. God isn't working things out the way John expected. Jesus isn't living up to all John's ideas about what the Messiah would do. Maybe Jesus isn't who he claims to be. It's the same kind of doubt we experience, right there in the life of one of Scripture's heroes.

I love the honesty of John's doubt. But what I find even more interesting is Jesus' response. I think John wants Jesus to show up and tell him all is well. That's what I want when I feel overcome by doubt. But Jesus doesn't go to John. What does that mean? Why does Jesus just tell John's disciples to go back and remind him of what they've seen? Why doesn't Jesus go back and sit with John in prison and respond to his questions?

> DOES DOUBT MEAN A PERSON'S FAITH IS IMMATURE? WHAT CAUSES YOU TO DOUBT GOD?

The answer is...we have no idea. Jesus, knowing John needs certainty, reminds John of what John already knows about Jesus. Was that enough? Was Jesus' power proof enough for John? Was Jesus sending John an entirely different message? Did he somehow understand John's heart and know John had a deeper question he hadn't told anyone?

It'd be easy to go on. I could spend hours imagining John's desperate doubt and wondering what Jesus is doing here. This is one of those Bible stories where I can't help but infuse who I am and what I'd need into the story. If I were John, I'd want Jesus to talk things out...to tell me what the deal was, why he hadn't teleported back to cure me of my doubt. I've always wanted God to be a talker...just like me. I've wanted him to talk through things with me—the direction of my life, how to parent my kids, what to do about our money problems, where we should go on vacation. Does it sound silly to say I want God to be my buddy? That I want him to sit with me over coffee, listen to me and say "uh huh" and "I hear what you're saying," and then tell me what to do?

I don't think so. I talk to God, and I want him to talk back. If God knows me the best and loves me the most, doesn't he know that's what I need?

HOLDING ON

WAS IT WRONG FOR JOHN TO DOUBT JESUS? WHAT DO YOU DO WHEN YOU NEED ASSURANCE FROM GOD?

I remember a time early in our marriage when Jacqui and I most wanted to hear God's voice and feel his presence.

Jacqui got pregnant soon after we were married. The pregnancy was unplanned, both of us were in school, and we weren't really ready to be parents. But the minute we learned she was pregnant, we began to dream about what our child might be like. We bought a few baby clothes. We started thinking about how much room we'd need to make in our tiny student apartment. We prayed for the baby growing inside her and that we would be good parents...good stewards of this tiny life given into our care.

Nothing really prepares you for losing a baby. There's the biology of the whole thing...some blood, a test or two, and the clinical discovery that there is no heartbeat. But there's also the whole emotional side, the response. In our case, it was deep sorrow. The life that had begun growing unexpectedly had become our hope for the next chapter of our lives. The miscarriage meant that chapter was not ready to be lived. With each passing day, we felt the loss more. The more we felt the loss, the more our pain grew. The more the pain grew, the more questions we had. Why was this happening? What had we done wrong? Did God hate us?

Just as I'd done during my time in the desert, we threw these questions at God—and never heard back from him. It felt a lot like sending emails to an old friend who never even bothers to send back a simple "Got your note. Yeah, that has to hurt." I felt empty and I felt angry, and honestly, I'm still angry.

And then, after our daughter Nicole was born, we experienced another pregnancy that ended in a miscarriage. Again we spent time asking questions. And again, God's silence was undeniably loud. Why was he choosing not to talk to us? Why was he letting us live alone in our pain? Was pleasure always followed by pain?

At the deepest place of who I am, this contradiction between the stated nature of God and his real nature still causes me to doubt, still sometimes makes me want to run away from him. When I read Scripture, I read about a God who loves his creation. Why would a God who loves us choose silence over our comfort? Why wouldn't he answer? I struggle with God's faithfulness. I struggle with his silence. And sometimes I just want to give up.

But maybe listening to God isn't just about hearing his voice. What if it's also about hanging on and not letting go through the silence? We don't know why

DOES THE IDEA THAT WE SHOULD HOLD ON EVEN WHEN WE DOUBT FEEL LIKE A CONCILIATORY STATEMENT? IS IT REALISTIC FOR US TO EXPECT THAT WE WILL HANG ON TO GOD THROUGH HIS SILENCE? IS IT A SIN IF WE DON'T?

God is silent. But maybe, whether we hear his voice or not, we need to hang onto him. We choose to hold on, even in the silence. Do we do this rationally, thinking logically, promising that we will not give up on God, that we will journey though his silence? I don't really know.

Positive and affirming words: *I choose to hold on in the silence.* I'll try to make them my own. Set up a dwelling in the quiet, and stay there, waiting, until I can hear his voice again. My hunger to hear drives me to wait. I believe that on some days, I will imagine myself in prayer, clinging at his feet, holding on to them with my arm wrapped so tightly around his ankles that his feet might turn blue. Other days, I'll be 20 steps away, with my back turned and my arms crossed.

I want to come to the place in my relationship with God that this promise is real in my life. I want to mean it, like the Jewish prisoner who wrote these words on the wall of his Auschwitz prison camp...

I believe in the sun, even when it is not shining.

I believe in love, even when I am alone.

I believe in God, even when he is silent.

I want to hold on, even when the pain is the most real, even when it is God's silence that screams the loudest.

CHAPTER TEN

BECOMING THE AUTHENTIC CHURCH

I'm sitting here thinking about the church, and I've got the television on. There's a televangelist on my screen. It's as if God knew I needed a little extra inspiration for this chapter—and guided me right to this channel.

I almost never watch Christian broadcasting. Usually, it just doesn't make sense to me. The preachers always seem to be begging for money, putting a price tag on God. The theology proclaimed on most Christian television programs always seems too trite and salesman-ish. Everything I love about Jesus feels like it's for sale on Christian television.

Honestly, I have no idea why this program is even on right now. I probably turned my attention to the television in a moment of writer's block, starting flicking through the channels, and stopped when I saw one of Jesus' Top Sellers, shilling for his latest revelation. He's preaching right now, standing on a red carpet and surrounded by several levels of people sitting in a horseshoe arrangement. And, I've got to say, I agree with most of what he's saying (which is rare for me). But the way he's saying it sounds like a used car salesman. You know those guys who spot you a mile away and run up and start talking. Before you know it, you need what they're selling—not because you're convinced but because they know how to sell. And this dude isn't really selling Jesus at all. He's selling prosperity. Apparently, God wants me to be rich, and it's a sin to be poor and in need.

This is one of those moments when I wish we had an original audio recording of Jesus preaching. Did he sound anything like this guy on TV right now? Did he sell himself? Did he size up the crowd and choose his words carefully so they'd all buy in, empty their pockets, and fund his next trip along the shores of Galilee?

But before we talk more about Jesus, let me say a little more about this television preacher. I don't mean to judge him. I'm certain that God doesn't want us judging one another. When I was first introduced to Christ, the phrase went something like this: "You shouldn't judge people, but you can inspect their fruit." Well, I'm not even sure about that. But I do feel like part of our responsibility as Christians is to speak up about those things in the world and in our communities that don't resonate with our souls. And maybe that's especially important when it comes to people like this television preacher, who claim to be speaking for God.

As I watch this guy, I find myself thinking that the best measure of who we are privately—who we are before God and God alone—is who we are in public. Our public lives reflect what we really believe and what is most important to us.

If that is true (and I think it is), then what can I learn from this television preacher about who he is? Does he really believe that hawking Jesus like a salesman is the best method for helping people experience God's grace? Does he really feel his ministry is so important that everyone should stop giving money to their local churches and other important causes and begin giving to him?

I believe this connection between our public lives with one another and our private lives before God is one of the cornerstones of Jesus' message. He stressed authenticity not just in private before God, but corporate authenticity—who we are together, how we treat one another, what we are as a body before God. Jesus knew that the two fit hand-in-glove. I bring the private me into the community of believers. And that, by the way, is part of the reason some of us feel so tempted to put on a mask in worship. We may come to the body wrecked and broken on the inside, but we'll mask it all with smiles and happy handshakes. But we're not doing the church any favors by pretending everything is okay. The wrecked and broken parts of us still affect God's church. That hidden self that we try to mask will slowly seep into the body and change it. Underneath the masks, my ick spreads and becomes your ick, and we live that together—always hiding it, denying it is there. And then we wonder why it's such a struggle for us to be the body of Christ.

PREACHERS AND PRACTICE

This isn't a new theme. The authenticity of the church was central to the message and ministry of Jesus. While Jesus certainly preached a message of repentance over and over to those outside the church, he also took direct aim at the authenticity of those who ran the church of his day. He had strong words for the Pharisees and other religious leaders. He criticized their religiosity. He took aim, over and over, at their empty ceremonialism. He challenged the way they robbed the poor and made the sacrificial system inaccessible.

WHAT'S THE BEST WAY TO HELP THE PEOPLE OF GOD EXPERIENCE GOD'S GRACE IN CHURCH?

Jesus held the community of the Pharisees accountable for their lack of authenticity. Take this passage from Matthew 23, where Jesus instructs his followers to be wary of religious leaders who don't follow their own teachings:

> The teachers of the law and the Pharisees sit in Moses' seat. So you must be careful to do everything they tell you. But do not do what they do, for they do not practice what they preach. They tie up heavy, cumbersome loads and put them on other people's shoulders, but they themselves are not willing to lift a finger to move them. Everything they do is done for peo-

ple to see...they love the place of honor at banquets and the most important seats in the synagogues; they love to be greeted with respect in the marketplaces and to have people call them "Rabbi." (23:2-7)

A few verses later, Jesus begins speaking directly to the Pharisees, saying things like...

Woe to you, teachers of the law and Pharisees, you hypocrites! You shut the door of the kingdom of heaven in people's faces. You yourselves do not enter, nor will you let those enter who are trying to. (23:13-14)

And...

Woe to you, teachers of the law and Pharisees, you hypocrites! You give a tenth of your spices—mint, dill and cumin. But you have neglected the more important matters of the law—justice, mercy and faithfulness. You should have practiced the latter, without neglecting the former. (23:23)

And...

Woe to you, teachers of the law and Pharisees, you hypocrites! You are like whitewashed tombs, which look beautiful on the outside but on the inside are full of the bones of the dead and everything unclean. In the same way, on the outside you appear to people as righteous but on the inside you are full of hypocrisy and wickedness. (23:27-28)

Now we need to remember that the Pharisees were among the most well trained religious leaders of Jesus day. They'd given their lives to studying God's word. And yet, Jesus tells them they are missing the point.

The Pharisees weren't a group of men dead set against everything Jesus represented. I think they welcomed the idea of the Messiah, but Jesus clearly wasn't the Messiah they'd hoped he would be. They came by their expectations honestly. They had been waiting through what's often called the "silent period" in Israel's history—the time between Jesus birth and the fall of Jerusalem about 500 years earlier when God was virtually silent to human ears. In that silence, people began holding on to what they knew: What God had done in Egypt, what he had said through the prophets, and what he promised he would do through the Messiah. The religious systems developed by the Pharisees were an effort to remind the people of their history, and help them connect with God in a time when he felt so distant. But the result was a religious structure filled with formalities that often kept people away from God.

That's what Jesus is addressing in his comments to the Pharisees. The structures they'd set up to stay connected to God no longer connected with the heart of God. Over time, ceremony and performance had become the focus. The passion that had once been an effort to reach the heart of God was now reaching lower, into the pockets of other believers, and out into the religious system, seeking to change it for their own interests.

Sometimes it feels the exact same way today. In our own pursuit of corporate authenticity, we in the church have to admit that we're not too unlike the Pharisees in Jesus' day. We love the ceremony. We live for the great old songs, we want what we've had in the past, or we desire to noodle with the past and create something new, something of our own hands. We want what God has been, but we too often do not want what he could be in our churches. We've got things in order, and that's enough. But we don't really want Jesus to show up. That would be too much.

DO YOU THINK JESUS WOULD SAY THESE SAME KINDS OF THINGS TO CHURCH LEADERS TODAY? WHY OR WHY NOT?

Consider the contrast between Jesus' words for the Pharisees and the descriptions of the early Christian church in the Book of Acts. After Jesus rose, promised the Holy Spirit, and disappeared, believers banded together to form what Paul would later call the body of Christ—the church. Listen to this description of the early believers from Acts 2:42-47…

> They devoted themselves to the apostles' teaching and to fellowship, to the breaking of bread and to prayer. Everyone was filled with awe at the many wonders and signs performed by the apostles. All the believers were together and had everything in common. They sold property and possessions to give to anyone who had need. Every day they continued to meet together in the temple courts. They broke bread in their homes and ate together with glad and sincere hearts, praising God and enjoying the favor of all the people.

And the Lord added to their number daily those who were being saved.

And this one, from Acts 4:32-35...

All the believers were one in heart and mind. No one claimed that any of their possessions was their own, but they shared everything they had. With great power the apostles continued to testify to the resurrection of the Lord Jesus. And God's grace was so powerfully at work in them all that there were no needy persons among them. For from time to time those who owned land or houses sold them, brought the money from the sales and put it at the apostles' feet, and it was distributed to anyone who had need

IN WHAT WAYS DO YOU SEE THE CHURCH STUCK IN CEREMONY TODAY? WHAT WOULD JESUS SPEAK A "WOE" AGAINST TODAY?

Take some time to go back and read Jesus' words from Matthew, and then reread those words from Acts. As you read the two passages from Acts, underline the words and phrases that represent what you think the authentic church looks like. My favorite words are *awe, give, ate together, God's grace*, and *distributed to anyone*.

Those two passages from Acts cause me to think that, somehow, at its inception, the church really understood the core of what Jesus called us to. Those closest to the story understood the heart of their teacher and were deeply motivated to live out his call together, regardless of the struggles they'd face.

I know that it's easy to cite these two brief passages from Acts, point back to the early days of the church, and wonder why we're not like that. And if we knew the whole story, we might find out that there were money-grubbing power-seekers in the church back then, just as there are now. Still, I think maybe those two passages aren't just there as history—to tell us what the church was like back then. Maybe they're included in the Scriptures to help us see what we're supposed to become. Maybe those passages are there by God's hand because he wants us to see his vision for his church today.

Is it too easy for me to say that God's purpose for the church today is exactly what it was when the early believers lived? Is it just finger-pointing to suggest that many of our churches have more in common with the Pharisees than the church described in Acts? Is it too much to say that we're overly concerned with building churches into empires? Is it even possible for us to return to studying and living out the simple teachings of Jesus the way the early Christians did?

A VISION FOR THE BODY OF CHRIST

Now I understand that holding up the early church might seem overly simplistic. But I do believe it's been set in front of us the ideal, as a vision of what we could be. And it's a vision that affects us on two related levels—both our inner, individual pursuit of authenticity and our corporate authenticity as the body of Christ.

When I start asking myself questions about the body of Christ, about what it means to be authentic *together* as the church, the questions become pretty

IS IT REALISTIC TO THINK CHURCHES TODAY CAN BE MORE LIKE THE COMMUNITY OF BELIEVERS DESCRIBED IN ACTS? WHAT MIGHT NEED TO CHANGE FOR OUR CONGREGATIONS TO BECOME MORE LIKE THE EARLY CHURCH?

uncomfortable. It's easy to fall into the trap of thinking of church primarily as a place you go on Sunday mornings. And that can quickly lead to thinking of attending church as a chore. We might go to church out of ceremony, or because we've always gone, or because we've been raised going. Maybe we go because our parents love going there (and want us to love it) or because all our friends are there. Or maybe we're there out of guilt—we're concerned about what others might say if we're not there or about what our sleeping in on Sunday might say about our spiritual lives.

Personally, I want my connection to the church to be more than an obligation. I want my church attendance to flow from a desire to connect with God in the body he's called me to. I want to go because there's biblical teaching there that deepens my roots, because there's music that speaks to my soul, because worship helps me connect with God. I want my tithing to be an act of faith and worship, not an opportunity to help fill up the church budget. I want to go for the connections, not the coffee. I guess I'm saying that I want to want to be a part of that worshipping community. If I don't have that desire, it feels inauthentic to attend.

But being the church is more than just showing up on Sunday mornings. I want to be connected with the rest of the body. I want friendships within the church that are based on my desire to be present with Jesus, not present with my friends. Or, to say it another way, if I go to church mainly to be with my friends, and the worship service is just the place where we make that connection, it feels wrong to me. That makes God an extra. Instead, I want to be drawn into the presence of Christ first, and to connect with others because we share that desire to be in relationship with God. I should ask questions like, "Where do I most experience Christ?" and, "Where can my gifts be used best?" before I ask, "Where do my friends go?" I hope that who I am can best be used where my best friends attend, but I'm not always certain that will be true.

Authentic participation in the body of Christ also means rethinking our devotion to that body. In recent years, I haven't participated very actively in the building of my own church's structure and programming. Now part of my reason for that is my own effort to live authentically, to be honest about who I am—and I am a guy who truly can't stand structures and programs. But if I say that I'm part of this local expression of the body of Christ, then I need to actively participate in that body. It doesn't mean going to every activity. But it does mean involving myself in the life of the body. It means voicing my opinion when I agree and disagree with its direction. It means realizing I have a unique role to play within that body, and that the body is incomplete without me.

WHERE IS GOD?

It's so easy to believe God is found only within our church building. We pray that way, don't we? We stand at the beginning of worship and ask God to be with us in our worship there, like the sanctuary is the only place where God dwells. But as part of my own authentic journey, I want to remember that Jesus is everywhere; he's inside the church as we worship, moving and living and breathing along with us, and he's outside the church, walking alongside us, encouraging us forward into moments of genuine worship.

And how does that authentically translate in our lives? I think it means we can worship God everywhere and anywhere. Worship can happen in any place, in any situation. It can happen when we are alone, and when we are gathered with others. If we are outside and singing, worship can happen—and God is there. If we are alone at night thinking about God, worship can happen. If we are watching a movie that deals with a spiritual topic, and that subject causes us to connect deeply with the heart of God, can't worship happen there? It blows my mind when I remember those moments of prayer I've had in my car or alone in my house where I've keenly felt God was in that space with me. It feels so unorthodox to say that, and yet, it feels wrong not to admit it.

WHAT'S YOUR MOTIVATION FOR ATTENDING CHURCH?

But the uncomfortable truth of all this is that our life together as the body of Christ isn't always pleasant...it's not all chocolate and flowers. I have my list of things that make me angry about the church, and I've already mentioned many of them. There are the TV preachers who seem focused on money over ministry and the political groups that co-opt Jesus for their own purposes. The frustrating theological debates that divide us—conflicts over predestination, or eternal security, or the role of the Holy Spirit. The way we use our power to picket the very same places Jesus would probably have entered to spread his love. The constant talk of being "at war" with anyone who doesn't agree with us, language that feels so far from the heart of God. The way we define our faith by what (and who) we are against instead of opening our doors wide and helping those who have never discovered God's love to find it.

I don't think all that represents the direction God wants us to lead in the world. I believe God's vision for his church is that we would be his authentic community *outside* the church walls, that we would be so active in meeting the needs of those who have never met Christ that they will want to discover what we have discovered. God's heart is not *against* anyone; it is *for* everyone—regardless of what we may have done. And that compassionate, forgiving heart of God is best demonstrated in the world by an authentic, loving community.

I still believe that community has to be rooted in authentic worship, This passion to be connected to others in God's body means crafting our worship services in ways that allow all kinds of believers to feel comfortable worshipping how they want, speaking and singing and moving in a way that reflects their own unique ways of praising God. When we are all free to worship in the way that we were uniquely created, authentic praise erupts.

I recently experienced this while on vacation with my wife and kids. On the way home from a week at camp together, we stopped to visit my sister. She attends worship services at a satellite campus for a larger church. It's an interesting situation, in which there's live worship in the building they're sitting in, but there's also worship that gets piped in from the main campus. When I heard about this format, I was skeptical. It felt like I was showing up to watch others worship on television.

WHAT CREATES AUTHENTIC COMMUNITY AMONG BELIEVERS? HOW DO YOU CONTRIBUTE TO COMMUNITY IN YOUR CHURCH?

But when we walked through the doors of this "church," there were business executives talking with pierced teenagers. There were seniors keeping a watchful eye on the preschoolers who were running around. There were people from all walks of life, sipping coffee and talking with one another. It didn't feel like church, it felt like a redemptive community gathering together around their love for God. I knew something good was going on, and I understood the core of what brought them together as we began the worship service. The music for the service was provided by a live band there in the room. Some of us sat and drank coffee as they played, others stood and clapped, and others did a slow dance groove. As the message was piped in from the main campus, some folks cheered and laughed and applauded, while others sat silently, in awe of the message.

It didn't sound like my kind of worship before I entered that room, but what I experienced there sure felt like worship. And one of the beauties of that environment was that there were no boundaries on what we could do in God's presence. I'm not a dancing-in-worship kind of guy, but I know that if I'd chosen to dance, no one would have minded. In fact, I suspect a conga line would have formed behind me. It wasn't an "anything goes" environment, but it was a "God accepts everyone, just as they are" environment. True worship was the core motivator for strong community. It was beautiful.

REAL COMMUNITY

Authentic community happens when all of us come together as we seek to live a life of love before God and glorify him with our lives. It happens when we realize that accepting each person's individuality is the cornerstone of good community.

> HOW DOES OUR BEING AUTHENTIC AS INDIVIDUALS CONTRIBUTE TO AUTHENTIC COMMUNITY?

This past year in the biblical studies classes I teach at the local university, I reached a fairly critical moment. For years I'd been teaching the same curriculum in the same way, encouraging students to adopt my own ideas and philosophy. I was teaching in a way that urged them to accept that I was right about everything—the text we were examining, the theology we were exploring, and the methods needed for good hermeneutical Bible study.

But late last summer, before classes started, I had a realization that was fueled by my reading of those passages from the Sermon on the Mount in Matthew. I realized I was doing a lot of talking in class and wasn't facilitating much discussion. I said I was teaching people to think on their own, but I'd grown fairly adept at just teaching students to think like me.

IN WHAT WAYS DO
YOU STRUGGLE WITH
SAMENESS?

I didn't throw out the old curriculum, but I tossed out the way I taught it. Instead of teaching to help students better understand my thinking, I sought to create a place where students could share their own beliefs, talk about their passion for (or hatred of) Bible study, and discuss the core of their own faith. Classes on the trinity led down beautiful roads, considering a range of models and understandings of the trinity. Discussions on the nature and character of God became conversation about the wonder of all we really do not know about God. We dipped to the right and left, and sometimes veered off the path of orthodox belief and into some gray areas.

Several students told me that class helped them go deeper in their walks with God. But, maybe more importantly (if there is anything more important than that), after a few heated discussions about crucial issues where our beliefs differed, we came to understand that it's okay to be in a room of believers who don't agree about everything. We understood that belief is intensely personal, but that intensity doesn't mean we don't ever discuss what we believe or listen to someone who thinks differently. We came to understand that community isn't created when we all pretend to believe the exact same thing, it's created when we get together and hash out what we believe, in love, in the presence of God.

I feel like so much of what passes for community in today's church world is built around sameness. Large churches group people together based on similar ages, interests, or life stages. Connections happen and community love for God is developed, but in my experience, it's more often by accident rather than any set programming. Yet authentic community is built on individuality, and it's built when every individual is his or her true self.

This quest to be part of an authentic community of believers has had a deep impact on my life. I've always valued authenticity, and I've often felt like the church today was too often like the Pharisees of Jesus' day. But where does that leave me? What does that mean for my life as part of the body of Christ? How does my lack of authenticity affect the church I belong to? And, more pointedly for me as a youth pastor, how does my lack of authenticity affect my ministry and the teenagers I work with?

IF JESUS WERE SPEAKING TO YOUR CHURCH CONGREGATION TODAY, DO YOU THINK HIS WORDS WOULD SOUND MORE LIKE THOSE HE SPOKE TO THE PHARISEES OR LIKE THOSE HE SPOKE TO THE DISCIPLES IN MATTHEW 28?

I've had to face those questions as I've written this chapter—and this entire book. And the closer I looked at the Pharisees, the more I saw myself in them. Their ceremonialism and focus on an outward display of their faith was too much like mine. Their addiction to rules mirrored my own love for boundary-creating laws. I saw myself in the way they fixated on religious structures instead of the heart of God.

That's a hard thing to come to terms with, especially when you're the "expert" writing a book about authenticity before God. When who you are doesn't match up with who you say you want to be, you're not left with too many options. And, for me, there was only one way to take a step away from the inauthentic person I'd become. There was only one thing I could do if I really wanted to be authentic, to find a place that was healthier for me and for the youth I've been working with. And so, around the time I finished writing this book, I quit my job working at the church—allowing the church to move someone less pharisaical into that position and allowing God to begin a new work inside me.

This search for authenticity is a hard one. It can lead us to make some difficult, life-shaping decisions. Right now, I have no idea where God will lead me in terms of my next job. But I clearly understand that this decision to move on was God's healthy choice for me.

I think sometimes God leads us to a place that feels like the end for us, but it is really just a new beginning to him. I wonder if that's where I am now. But, all things considered, I'd rather be unemployed than be a Pharisee.

CHAPTER
LONGING
ELEVEN

We'd been out all day doing our Christmas shopping. Jake got a bike. Jess got a handheld gaming system. Nicole got a stereo. And I didn't get lunch—and dinner was still a long way off. "Honey," I said, with a low voice somewhat weakened by hunger, "can't we please stop now for a quick something to eat? Just a hamburger, or even just fries? Something quick, before my body starts to turn into water?" But Jacqui, in full "shop till you drop" mode, said we needed to keep going. We finally arrived home a few hours later. I ate my belly back into fatness, satisfying my craving and giving my body what it needed.

I have a love affair with food, and I'm actually kind of particular about the kind of food I love. I don't do seafood, I'm not a fan of undercooked meats, and I'm not typically adventurous. But, when I'm hungry, it affects everything about me. I can't think. I'm grumpy and impatient. Over time, my family has learned they need to make sure I eat on time. I'm a lot easier to be around.

WHAT WILL YOU DO TODAY TO CONNECT WITH GOD?

Even as I tell you about how I can't stand being physically hungry, I realize that I'm willing to go long periods of time without any kind of spiritual meal. I might crave a plate of mashed potatoes, but I don't seem to crave that deeper connection to God—at least not the way I wish I did. I feel sad about that, as if I've failed you somehow. You get all the way to the end of this book on authentic spirituality only to have me admit that, even though I believe hunger for God is tremendously important, in my own life, the actual experience of truly craving God, of longing for his presence, is somewhat rare.

I have no idea how God works in all this. Is it like math? If we do X, Y, and Z, then God responds by showing up? Do we strive for holiness our entire lives and then we finally encounter God? How desperate do I have to be before God steps into the portrait of my life?

Honestly, it's so frustrating to watch others who seem to connect with God so freely and easily, and then have to admit that truly experiencing God's presence in my own life is so unusual that, when it does happen, I feel like starting a parade around my house and letting everyone know I've had "one of those moments." Those times when I really have an experience of God stand out to me like shining moments. And yet, I still don't seem to seek God with the kind of urgency I wish I had, the urgency I see in others. One day, I hope my own passion for God will take such deep root that it'll be like the longing I see in Moses here...

Moses said to the Lord, "You have been telling me, 'Lead these people,' but you have not let me know whom you will send with me. You have said, 'I know you by name and you have found favor with me.' If you are pleased with me, teach me your ways so I may know you and continue to find favor with you. Remember that this nation is your people."

The Lord replied, "My Presence will go with you, and I will give you rest."

Then Moses said to him, "If your Presence does not go with us, do not send us up from here. How will anyone know that you are pleased with me and with your people unless you go with us? What else will distinguish me and your people from all the other people on the face of the earth?"

And the Lord said to Moses, "I will do the very thing you have asked, because I am pleased with you and I know you by name."

Then Moses said, "Now show me your glory."

And the Lord said, "I will cause all my goodness to pass in front of you, and I will proclaim my name, the Lord, in your presence. I will have mercy on whom I will have mercy, and I will have compassion on whom I will have compassion. But," he said, "you cannot see my face, for no one may see me and live."

Then the Lord said, "There is a place near me where you may stand on a rock. When my glory passes by, I will put you in a cleft in the rock and cover you with my hand until I have passed by. Then I will remove my hand and you will see my back; but my face must not be seen." (Exodus 33:12-23)

I love Moses' deep desire to really see and know the God he serves. I want that same kind of passion. I don't want to walk into God's presence the same way I stride into my favorite burger joint for another French fry fix. I want Moses' passion. I want to cry out: "Now show me your glory." In my life I have never really prayed that—but I want to. I *want* to have that kind of desire. I want God to fill me with that passion for him. I don't have that kind of desire, but I want to have that desire. I'm not that interested in God, but I *want* to be that interested in God.

I think that's the real motivation for my wanting to write this book about authenticity. As I finish writing, I wonder…have I spent the entirety of this book just trying to say that I want what Moses had? Are all the different issues in this book just a series of foothills I had to journey over to get to that real mountain of a question: How passionately do we really want to be like Jesus?

THE LIMITS OF LANGUAGE

Words are what a writer has to share his or her heart, yet sometimes they feel so limiting. If you and I were sitting together over a sandwich, I'd probably use a lot more than words. I'd use gestures. Inflection. Faces. I'd use everything I could to help you understand why I feel this struggle for authenticity is so important.

DO YOU FIND YOURSELF ENTERING GOD'S PRESENCE TOO CASUALLY?

But we're not talking over lunch. I'm writing this book and you're reading it, and words are all we have. Yet they fail to fully express what is happening inside me. They fail in describing my hunger for God—and the times when I don't hunger for God. They don't feel adequate for the task of telling you about my passion, and the passion you should have for Jesus. I want to say things like, "Live your love for God dangerously"—but even as I say that, I'm concerned that those words get it wrong. They don't say enough. They don't say it right.

I find that frustration not just in writing this book but in my relationship with God. There is so much going on inside me. My love for him. My questions. My fears. My passion to know more. My doubts. Everything that is me. And each of those things I just listed has a bunch of *abouts* attached to it, like "My fears *about* my future" and "My questions *about* what heaven is like" and "My love for God even though I really don't understand much *about* him." I want so much for you to understand this longing clearly, like you're seeing it through a crystal clear window. I want the questions and uncertainties, all that is unfinished in me, to be so obvious to God and so clear to the people I love, so that my passion, while wavering at times, can continue to grow.

It's interesting that we never hear Moses try and describe what he saw that day when he saw God's glory. As much as is recorded in Scripture about Moses and his relationship with God, there's never any description from Moses about what he saw that day. Come to think of it, Moses never describes any of his one-on-one encounters with God. Remember those times when he went outside the community to convene with God at the tent of meeting? We never hear Moses talk about what he's seen. I wonder if that's because Moses felt the same way about the limitations of language in describing God and our relationship with him. Why try and describe the presence of the Creator when your words will never do justice to what you've seen and felt? I bet Moses understood this. It's impossible to explain the Almighty. And finding words for our own pursuit of God falls in the same category. How do we put words around the on-and-off passion we feel? How do we describe those moments when we struggle to touch just the corner of God's clothes? What do we say about our efforts to follow Christ and our ability to fall backward into sin or our struggle to love people who hate God?

I believe that if we live the way we really want to live, if our lives are rooted in the God who pushes past all our boundaries, then words will never be enough. Words like *love* and *faith* and *passion* and *hope* and *hunger* and so many others will point toward the reality, but they will never capture it. The words will feel too small, too flat, too empty. We may use them, but even then we'll know that those words do not work. We may say passion, but the word can't really express our desire for God. We might talk about God's love, but that doesn't begin to express all God has done for us. Our passion for God, if it truly is passion for God—and not for ourselves or money or prestige or popularity or something else— will constantly push us upward and outward toward him.

That's real desire. And it's the result of a passion that reaches that far up and outside of us. If our souls truly crave to know God, those cravings will come out in all kinds of expressions. In tears. In silence. In words we make up. In movements we make with our hands and body. In drawings and other expressions of creativity. I want to release myself into those expressions because I believe that words do not adequately express my spiritual quest toward God. Words are useful for part of my expression, but they don't even begin to express the agony or the joy of my walk with God. Sometimes I prefer not to talk about my walk, because the moment I use finite words to express my infinite journey I have reduced the immeasurable to something measurable. I have taken something that lives and breathes and moves and made a plastic replica of it.

Desire and passion should move us forward in our authentic struggle. We're gonna fail, but who cares? This journey isn't about living perfectly; it's about

> WHAT COULD YOU USE BEYOND WORDS TO EXPRESS YOUR PASSION FOR GOD? WHAT WOULD YOU MOST WANT TO COMMUNICATE?

moving forward in Christ. It's not about becoming the perfect poster children for the next generation of young believers. It's about the passionate desire to connect with Jesus, to live like him.

We'll continue to question what it means to live like Jesus. We're going to wonder if we're focusing on too many surface things. We'll wonder if we're really supposed to love the person we struggle to like, and we'll wonder if Jesus would want to tell that guy off as much as we want to. We'll still have as many questions about God as we have answers. But that's all part of the desire and passion in us that moves us forward in godliness.

DO YOU THINK YOU SHOULD BE ABLE TO PUT YOUR PASSION FOR GOD INTO WORDS? IF YOU CAN'T DO THAT, DOES IT MEAN YOU ARE LESS SPIRITUAL?

So as you get ready to close this book, I don't want to suggest three quick things you need to do or imply that there's any simple recipe for authenticity. Instead, I want to invite you to journey with me, to seek God (and want to seek him) with your entire life. I want to invite you to set aside any rules you've been taught about what right living is and seek to live as Jesus would live today. I invite you to live the desire that is in you to be in God.

You see, authenticity isn't about getting everything in your life right. It's about passionately pursuing God instead of our desire to be right. It's about loving Jesus instead of loving the made-up stuff that comes with trying to love Jesus.

The more that you and I do that, the more we will grow into a community of people seeking an authentic relationship with Jesus. The more we do that, the more we will impact each other in our journey toward godliness.

I know that as I've searched for my own authentic faith, I've been significantly impacted by the people I love and the way I see them journeying with Jesus. I've been changed by the lives and the faith of so many people around me. My mentors when I was younger. My wife's parents, and especially her dad, who continues his quest toward God despite his Alzheimer's. My grandparents-in-law, who, at age 97, continue faithfully lifting up our family in prayer. My pastor, who always seems able to drop everything else in his life when someone else needs him. My students, like the young Mormon woman who continues to love and serve God and doesn't care that others think some of her beliefs are completely crazy. My friend who can recite entire chapters of Paul's writings and has made it his goal to memorize the entire New Testament. My cousin who works with kids in Africa and retains hope despite the incredible poverty and sickness he sees every day. These are just some of the people whose lives have shaped mine. It's not that they've used the right words to tell me about their spiritual lives or their experiences of God. They have just lived, letting me observe their lives as if I'm watching a delicate ballet.

> WHAT PEOPLE CLOSE TO YOU WILL BE MOST AFFECTED BY YOUR AUTHENTICITY? WHAT CAN YOU DO TODAY TO ENCOURAGE YOUR FAMILY AND FRIENDS IN THEIR OWN WALKS WITH GOD?

Their longing for God is beautiful. It is obvious. I see it, and I am filled with spiritual envy—wanting what they have, and hoping to find some shortcut that will make me more like them. Too often I find myself asking, "How did they get there?" instead of "Who do I need to be?"

AS YOU CLOSE THIS BOOK, YOU ARE BEGINNING THE NEXT STEP ON YOUR JOURNEY TOWARD BECOMING THE PERSON GOD CREATED YOU TO BE. WHAT WILL YOU DO NEXT?

I think my quest toward being godly, toward being the person God calls me to be, begins right here at home. Because my walk with God isn't something that affects only me. It shapes the people closest to me. It shapes Jacqui and her walk with God. It shapes my kids. The more spiritual I am, the more questing I am, the more I can see those same characteristics growing in them. This is not selfishness, and it is not male-dominant head-of-the-household stuff. It is truth. We affect the spiritual lives of those with whom we live in community. By living out my love for God, I help bring my family along in their own spiritual journeys.

Our family has been trying to gather together every night for prayer and Bible reading. We do this as a family because we want to remember that, whatever has happened that day, we want to end it rooted in God. We want to experience God as we close our good days and our bad ones. We want to take those moments when we are about to rest and devote them to God, so we can reflect on his goodness as we sleep. And we also do it because we believe Christians need to study the Bible, and Christian families should read it together.

In those family times, we sometimes take tangential trips down biblical roads. *What do you think John the Baptist smelled like?* or *Would you have given up your fish for 5,000 people?* are just a couple paths we've journeyed down recently. Sometimes those times are interrupted by frustrations over school or stress about the laundry or questions about a book someone has been reading. Some nights there are many interruptions. Some nights no one talks. And, in all honesty, these nights aren't filled with as many spiritual highs as I'd hoped for. In my mind, I imagined more would be happening. I imagined we'd feel more certain that God appreciates our efforts, that our attempts have his stamp of approval, and that he can really see the impact they are having on our lives.

I struggle with feeling caught between my desire to be a hero for my kids and my sense that I'm a failure before God. The truth is probably somewhere between the two, and I'm smart enough to know that focusing on one or the other isn't wise. In the end, I think God knows my heart, understands my longing, and is pleased by my desire to be authentically connected to him. I know that working it all out is something I will struggle with my entire life. Along the way, my hope is that my journey will be an encouragement to my friends, an example for my children, and an honest offering to God.

Understanding God's will in their lives can be over-whelming for teens. We know that God is calling them to change the world, but how are they supposed to do that? This book helps students know that they were created for a purpose, defines for them how to discover God's call, and encourages them to use that to change the world.

Leave a Footprint Change the Whole World

Tim Baker
Retail $9.99
978-0-310-27885-6

Visit www.youthspecialties.com
or your local bookstore.

youth
specialties